Why Is Milk White?

Why Is Milk White?

& 200
OTHER CURIOUS
chemistry
QUESTIONS

ALEXA COELHO & SIMON QUELLEN FIELD

CHICAGO
REVIEW
PRESS

Copyright © 2013 by Alexa Coelho and Simon Quellen Field
All rights reserved
First edition
Published by Chicago Review Press, Incorporated
814 North Franklin Street
Chicago, Illinois 60610
ISBN 978-1-61374-452-9

Library of Congress Cataloging-in-Publication Data
Is available from the Library of Congress.

Cover design: Andrew Brozyna, AJB Design, Inc.
Interior design: PerfecType, Nashville, TN

Printed in the United States of America
5 4 3 2 1

To Kari, Christian, and Clay

→ Contents

Preface

BY SIMON QUELLEN FIELD

I was talking one day with my coauthor, 11-year-old Alexa Coelho, about science, in particular about chemistry, which is her favorite subject. I was explaining that in much of science, the hard part is coming up with the right questions. Once you ask the right questions, half the work is done.

She had been reading a book that had two authors. One was a person with a special story to tell, and the other was a person who had written several books and knew how to put the right words onto paper to tell the story well. Alexa thought it might be fun to write a book but thought she would need some assistance from someone who knew the ins and outs of the publishing business. I agreed to help her in her endeavors.

Alexa then took the reins and worked very hard, without any assistance, doing the hard part of science. She spent almost all of her free time coming up with page after page of questions about chemistry that she wished she knew the answers to.

When she had come up with an astounding 200 questions about chemistry, she made me a gracious and generous offer. She would split the profits from her book 50/50 with me, if I would do the easy part and write the answers to the questions. I accepted her kind offer, and the result is this book.

Along with the addition of a few fun projects and a glossary, the questions got trimmed a bit, as happens during editing. But Alexa assures me that all of the important ones are still there.

How to Read Structural Formulas

Throughout this book, you'll see drawings that illustrate a particular chemical's *structural formula*—how it's shaped at a molecular level. Knowing its shape is often quite useful in understanding how it behaves and how it interacts with other compounds.

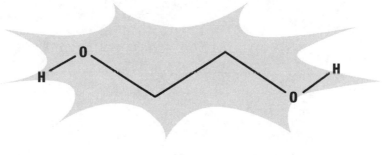

Structural formula for *ethylene glycol*

Chemists use a few simplifying rules to show how a molecule is shaped without cluttering up the picture. Most of the atoms that make up a molecule are labeled; in the structural formula above, hydrogen is labeled with an "H" and oxygen is labeled with an "O." But carbon atoms are so common that they are not labeled with a "C." Instead, they are assumed to be anywhere on a formula where two lines join, like the two middle bends in the above drawing.

And since hydrogens attached to carbons are also very common, and carbon always has four bonds, any place on a formula where fewer than four lines join, it is assumed that hydrogens fill the carbon's remaining bonds, and so they are not labeled either. That means that there are two more hydrogen atoms attached to each of the unlabeled carbons at the center of the formula on the previous page.

1

People and Animals

Though Alexa's questions are about her favorite subject, chemistry, it turns out that a lot of chemistry is involved in how people and animals react to their environment and how they grow, eat, and breathe.

Can chemicals cause mutations in animals?

Yes. But they won't turn you into Spider-Man.

Chemicals that cause mutations are called *mutagens*. Mutagens cause changes in the DNA in the cells of an organism. DNA is a code that spells out how to make things in a cell. The code is made up of letters like an alphabet. Each letter represents a different chemical, called a *nucleotide*. There are four letters in the DNA alphabet: A, C, G, and T.

But there are some molecules that look like one of the molecules DNA uses for letters in the code. When the cell makes new DNA, it might use one of the molecules that looks like a T (for example), so that instead of spelling ACTGGTACCT, the DNA spells ACXGGTACCT. That X is the new molecule.

Usually when a spelling error like this occurs, the cell detects it and throws that DNA away so nothing bad happens. But sometimes the molecule looks so much like the real-letter molecule that it goes undetected. The misspelled word usually just doesn't work, so the cell doesn't make the chemical (usually a protein) it was supposed to make.

If the missing chemical is important, the cell might die, and that would be the end of it. If the missing chemical was not so important, such as something that made hair dark, you might get a gray hair instead. If the cell was a fertilized egg, all the hairs in the new animal might be white, and you get an *albino*, an animal that lacks the dark colors that make suntans and dark hair.

Sometimes the spelling change does make a protein, but the protein is just slightly different. It might not work as well, or it might work differently, maybe making a different color, and you get a blue frog instead of a green one.

Other chemicals might change a C into a T. Or break DNA into pieces that get put back together in the wrong order, or with a piece missing, or an extra piece added.

The likelihood of a mutation being beneficial is very small. A cell is a complicated piece of machinery, and making random changes would be like making a random change to a car engine by hitting it with a rock. The engine is unlikely to work better afterward. But occasionally a change makes the organism work better. This is evolution.

What happens if you breathe in smoke or carbon dioxide?

Smoke is made up of carbon dioxide, carbon monoxide, water vapor, soot, and smaller amounts of many other molecules and bits of ash. Soot and ash are filtered by your nose and pushed out of your throat when you cough. Carbon monoxide is toxic because it binds to blood cells instead of oxygen and doesn't let go, so your cells can't get any oxygen to breathe.

Carbon dioxide is something we breathe all the time, since it is a part of the air we breathe out of our lungs. Our bodies sense how much carbon dioxide is in our blood, and when the levels rise, we feel the need to take a breath.

If you breathe in too much carbon dioxide, your blood becomes acidic, since carbon dioxide dissolves in water to form carbonic acid. After breathing too much carbon dioxide, your body adjusts by making you breathe faster, so you exhale more carbon dioxide. It is the buildup of too much carbon dioxide that makes you feel the intense need to breathe when you are holding your breath or swimming underwater.

What does biology have to do with chemistry?

Biological organisms are made of chemicals. Some branches of biology study how the chemicals in organisms do their jobs. The scientists who study the molecules of life are called *biochemists*.

There are many biologists who study aspects of living things that are not directly related to the molecules that make up the animal or plant. But since animals and plants are made up of molecules, even people who study animal behavior or classify plants will eventually find some chemistry is useful.

Suppose you were studying the behavior of butterflies. You might want to know how they find their food or how they find their mates. Both of these behaviors involve sensing molecules in the air using their antennae. That's chemistry.

Or maybe you want to study human nutrition. To understand why some foods are essential, you might want to learn about vitamins, minerals, proteins, fats, carbohydrates, and other chemicals that make up our food.

Charles Darwin studied biology and came up with the theory of evolution. But it was chemists who figured out how evolution works, many years after Darwin was no longer around.

Doctors used to give their patients mixtures of plant material or other things in attempts to cure or alleviate symptoms of

PROJECT: SMOKING HANDS

Materials

Protective goggles
A few drops of household ammonia
A few drops of muriatic acid (available
   at hardware stores and swimming
   pool supply houses)
Water
Small bowl
2 paper towels or cotton balls
Wastebasket or similar container (optional)

Adult supervision required

In the photo on the right, I bring my two bare hands together and press so hard that they start to smoke.

Well, at least it looks like that. What is really going on is a chemical reaction between two vapors. One vapor comes from dampening my left

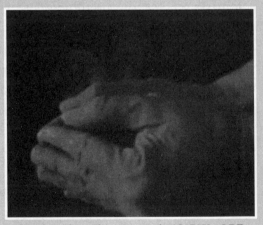

See the video at http://youtu.be/i21P1XzoLRE

hand with a little bit of household ammonia. The other vapor comes from dampening my right hand with a little diluted hydrochloric acid, known as muriatic acid. To try this yourself, combine a few drops of muriatic acid with twice as much water in a small bowl to further dilute it. ***Never use a more concentrated form of hydrochloric acid.*** Place a few drops of ammonia on a paper towel or cotton ball and wipe it onto your left palm. Use another paper towel or cotton ball to wipe the diluted muriatic acid onto your right palm. You should ***always wear protective goggles*** when handling these chemicals—which has the bonus of adding a dramatic sense of danger.

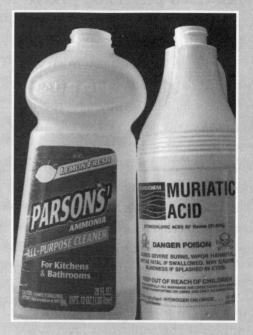

You don't want to do this unless your hands are free of cuts and scratches, as the hydrochloric acid will sting. But it does not attack the layer of dead skin on your palms, so despite the quite reasonable warnings on the bottle, it does no harm. Of course, it's also important to ***wash your hands well after the demonstration***. For those who quite sensibly want to avoid putting acid on their hands, the smoke effect can instead be done by placing a few drops of each solution on the paper towels or cotton balls and simply placing them near each other—say, in a wastebasket. Whichever technique you use, be careful to ***avoid breathing the vapors*** that result.

What is going on is a fairly simple chemical reaction. The ammonia solution releases ammonia gas (NH_3) into the air. The hydrochloric acid releases hydrogen chloride gas (HCl) into the air. The two gases react in the air to produce tiny particles of a white solid called ammonium chloride (NH_4Cl).

disease. But it was chemists who discovered how drugs work and how to find, extract, or make new ones.

As we learn more and more about life and about chemistry, the sciences of biology and chemistry have more and more to do with each other.

What does physiology have to do with chemistry?

While biology is the study of living things, physiology is the study of how living things work. Although many aspects of physiology have little to do with chemistry, it is hard to study how living things work without getting into chemistry somewhere.

You might be studying how light is focused in the eye, but eventually you get down to chemistry when you ask how the light gets turned into electrical signals to be sent to the brain. You might be studying how bacteria and viruses cause disease, but without a knowledge of chemistry you won't get very far.

Almost all of the Nobel Prizes in physiology and medicine were awarded for discoveries or inventions that deal with physiology at the molecular level in some respect.

Before studying physiology in medical school, it is strongly recommended that students first take chemistry courses, because so much of physiology depends on understanding how living things function at the molecular level.

How do we have hair?

Some of us don't. And most of us don't have hair on the bottoms of our feet, on our lips, on the palms of our hands, or on our eyelids, except along the very front edge, where we have eyelashes.

Each hair on your body grows in three stages. There is a growth stage, usually lasting two to three years (but sometimes as many as eight). This is followed by a two- to three-week period during which the hair stops growing and is cut off from its blood supply and from the cells that make new hair. After this comes a resting stage, lasting about three months. Then the cycle begins again, and a new hair pushes the old, dead hair out, and it falls away. Each hair has its own cycle, so only a few hairs are shed each day.

The timing of these three stages determines how long your hair will be. If the hair grows for a long time before it rests, the hair will be longer. The hair on your eyebrows only grows for about four to seven months and rests for about nine months, so the hairs there are not as long as those on the top of your head. The same timing of the growth and rest phases determines the length of the other hairs on your body.

Each person has different hair growth and rest cycles, determined by genetics and environmental factors. Some people can grow their hair very long, while others will find that their hair never gets much past their shoulders, even if they never cut it. Women can usually grow longer hair than men, because the hair growth cycles are affected by sex hormones.

Why are boys usually taller than girls?

Boys and girls are actually about the same height on average—until they reach the age of 12 or 13. After that age, girls' growth starts to level off. Boys continue growing until age 17 or 18.

Boys and girls grow about two inches per year until they reach puberty. Then they each have a growth spurt that lasts a year or two. During the growth spurts, boys grow a little faster than girls. Girls reach puberty (on average) about a year before boys do. Girls also end puberty earlier than boys. The differences in when they reach puberty, how fast they grow during it, and how long puberty lasts are what make boys average about five inches taller than girls by the time they stop growing.

To estimate how tall you will be when you are fully grown, you can use the knowledge that men are on average five inches taller than women. If you are a girl, subtract five inches from your father's height. Then add your mother's height, and then divide by two. This will give you the average height your parents would have if they were both women.

If you are a boy, add five inches to your mother's height, then add your father's height, and divide by two. This gives you the average height your parents would be if they were both men.

The problem with these estimates is that they will only let you guess your height within about four inches. That is a lot of variation. On average, siblings of the same sex will be within four inches of one another.

There is another way to estimate your adult height that indicates just how unreliable height estimation is. If you know how tall you were when you were two years old, you can double that to estimate your adult height. Notice that this method does not ask whether you are a boy or a girl. Remember that boys and girls grow at about the same rate until puberty, and that there is about a five-inch difference on average between men and women's height. So this estimate may easily be up to five inches off.

Why do people use lotion as a moisturizer?

Because they don't want dry skin. Skin acts as a barrier, preventing bad things from getting into the body but also preventing water in the body from evaporating away or leaking out.

The outermost layer of skin is made of dead cells. If these dead cells dry out too much, they can crack and separate, making holes in the protective barrier. Even if there are no cracks, the dry cells don't function as well, allowing moisture loss from the living cells below them.

Moisturizers generally have three types of ingredients. *Humectants* are molecules that absorb water from the air. Glycerin and urea are humectants, and you may see one or both of them on the label of your favorite lotion.

Emollients lubricate the skin and fill in the spaces between the dead cells to help make a better moisture barrier. They are generally oils, such as mineral oil, petroleum jelly, or lanolin. They also change the look and the feel of the skin in the same way that putting oil on paper makes the dry paper look transparent and wet.

The third type of ingredient will generally be some kind of preservative that prevents bacteria from degrading (damaging) the emollients and humectants.

Oil-free moisturizers are often used for areas like the face, which already have plenty of oil and where adding oil might cause acne. Moisturizers for knees and elbows will more likely have more oil than moisturizers for the face.

Some moisturizers improve the skin's natural barrier by adding a layer of oil, sunscreen, or antioxidants. These protect the skin from damage by sun, wind, and abrasion.

What kinds of chemicals do athletes drink before they do a race?

There are a number of supplements marketed to runners and cyclists to improve performance during races. How much they actually help may be more of an indication of the diet before the race or during training and of the mental state of the athlete than of any special powers of the ingredients. In other words, if the athlete is missing something, adding it back should help. And if the athlete believes the supplement will help, then the *placebo effect* (deceiving her into feeling better) may also improve performance.

Taking a lot of supplements before a race can actually harm performance if they cause digestive upset or other problems, and many of the supplements used have several negative side effects. A lot of coaches and professionals recommend doing nothing special for a race, only what you normally do during training.

Without making any recommendations or encouraging the use of supplements to improve performance, I can describe some of the supplements used and their claimed benefits.

Sodium phosphate or sodium bicarbonate is taken to buffer the lactic acid that builds up in muscles that are working without sufficient oxygen. Loading up on these before a race can cause digestive problems that lower performance.

Caffeine is taken as a stimulant. Drinking a couple cups of coffee is safe, but caffeine is a urinary stimulant, and stopping to pee will affect your race time.

Antioxidants such as vitamin E, beta carotene, selenium, and vitamin C are safe (though you *can* overdose on selenium, which affects insulin) and may help prevent some damage caused by strenuous exercise, but they won't help your performance in the race itself. And using too much may cause stomach upset.

Some people take supplements that relax the artery walls (*vasodilators*) under the impression that opening up the arteries increases blood flow to the muscles. But your body regulates your blood pressure carefully to make sure there is enough oxygen to the brain, and fainting during a race will affect your time. Being lightheaded generally does not improve performance in any activity, except possibly sleep. Combining vasodilators with dehydration is not a good idea.

Getting adequate salt for a long race can help prevent cramping. Some racers add magnesium and calcium as well. Loss of these electrolytes through sweat is one cause of cramps.

How has chemistry helped our health?

If you break your leg, it should be able to heal just fine without any chemical assistance other than a good diet. But you might feel better if you also take some acetylsalicylic acid (aspirin).

Other health problems can benefit more from a chemist's help. If you have a bacterial infection, some antibiotic chemicals that stop bacteria from growing, or kill the bacteria, might be a lot of help.

Knowledge of nutrition, which is the chemistry of what we eat, can also save lives and help people live longer. If you don't get a balanced diet or enough sun, then you might benefit from a chemist's knowledge of vitamins and minerals. Soap, toothpaste, acne medications, sunscreens, iodine, and chlorinated water all help keep you clean and free of infections.

But where chemistry really helps is when you have a serious health problem. Chemicals such as the insulin needed to treat diabetes or the antivirals used to treat HIV are lifesavers. Drugs to treat cancer, heart disease, and stroke can prolong lives by years.

On the other side of the coin, knowing which chemicals are dangerous can also save lives. The chemistry of poisonous substances (*toxicology*) helps keep us safe, but it also helps control pests that can affect our health, such as mosquitoes, rats and mice, cockroaches, and flies. Pesticides also increase crop yields, allowing more people to get the nutrition they need.

How is the human body related to chemistry?

We are made of chemicals. Understanding chemistry helps us understand our bodies and keeps us healthy.

Your bones are made of calcium phosphate. Your blood has iron in it to carry oxygen. The oxygen is needed for your cells to burn the glucose fuel they use for energy. The cells are enclosed in membranes made up of phospholipid molecules, and they function using enzymes made up of protein. More protein makes up your muscles, skin, and hair. Chemistry happens all throughout your body.

You can change the chemistry of your body. For example, the proteins in your hair can be changed to have more connections between them. This is done by adding chemicals to the hair to get a "permanent" wave to curl the hair. You can add fluorine to your teeth to make them less prone to cavities.

Why does Benadryl make you sleepy?

Benadryl contains the antihistamine diphenhydramine. The brain cells that are most concerned with wakefulness are the ones that release histamine, and these are the same brain cells that are targeted by antihistamines.

Histamine has many effects in the body. In the brain, it acts as a *neurotransmitter*, a chemical that sends signals between nerve cells.

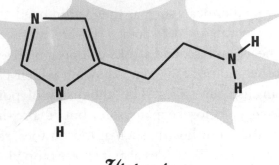

Histamine

It also causes the passageways in the lungs to constrict. It dilates blood vessels, allowing more blood to flow through them and lowering blood pressure. It is part of the immune system and is the cause of many of the symptoms you get when fighting off disease.

To help fight infections, histamine makes the small blood vessels leaky, so that white blood cells and antibodies can leak from the blood into the tissues to fight bacteria and viruses.

A side effect of leaky blood vessels is water leaking into tissues from the blood, causing runny noses and watery eyes. The enlarging of the small blood vessels causes swelling of tissue in places like the nasal passages, which then become blocked—a stuffy nose.

And histamine's other action, as a neurotransmitter, causes side effects when you have a cold. The nerves that detect sensation in your nose get stimulated, and you sneeze.

The action that makes the cells in the blood vessels loosen and leak can also affect skin cells, causing hives. The pain and itching of insect bites is due to histamine's effects on the skin and blood vessels as the body recognizes foreign proteins and attacks them.

To fight the symptoms of colds, allergies, and insect bites, we use antihistamines. But since histamine is a neurotransmitter that regulates wakefulness, a side effect of relieving cold symptoms is drowsiness.

There are four different types of histamine receptors in the body, and they control different reactions to histamine. Some new antihistamines target only one or two of these receptors, so they can relieve allergy symptoms without causing drowsiness.

Why do some people have dark skin and other people have light skin?

The main pigment in your skin is *melanin*. It protects your skin from damage caused by the rays of the sun. When you get more sun, your skin compensates by producing more melanin, and you get a tan.

But sunlight is needed to make vitamin D in your skin. So when people started living in northern countries that don't get as much sun as tropical countries do, they evolved to produce less melanin, so what little sunlight there was could get into the skin and produce enough vitamin D.

When ultraviolet light from the sun damages the DNA in your skin, the damage is detected and the skin produces more melanin. The melanin produced absorbs ultraviolet light very well and protects the DNA in the skin from further damage. If there is too much damage to the DNA, skin cancer can result.

Melanin is found in other places in the body besides the skin. It is the pigment that colors hair, and it is present in the iris of the eye. Even blue-eyed people usually have small areas of the iris that contain melanin.

There are many types of melanin, and they have different colors. Brown hair, black hair, blond hair, and red hair are colored by different amounts of the different types of melanin.

One type of melanin, *pheomelanin*, is pinkish or reddish and is what colors red hair. Another form, *eumelanin*, can be black or brown. If most of the melanin in hair is missing, except for a little bit of black eumelanin, you get gray hair. If most melanin is missing except for a little bit of brown eumelanin, you get blond hair.

Other animals also use melanin for coloration and protection from ultraviolet light. Octopi and squid use it to make the black ink they produce when attacked. Some bacteria and fungi use it as a sunscreen and as an antioxidant, and it can protect some micro-organisms from attack by a host animal's immune system.

2

Plants

All living things use chemistry, not just people and animals. A large part of the tree of life is the plant kingdom. Since plants can't run away or fight with tooth and claw, they have developed quite sophisticated chemical methods to get what they need or defend what they have.

Many of the chemical changes you see in plants have to do with their color. The leaves change color with the seasons, flowers come in bright colors to attract pollinators, and even the green of the leaves is due to the important chemistry involved with making sugar from water, air, and sunlight.

Do we get chemicals from plants?

We use plants mostly for food. Any industrial uses for plants would compete for land that could be growing food, or for food itself. Despite that, there are many industrial chemicals that are made from plants.

An example is the alcohol that is added to gasoline. Normal economics would prevent corn from being used to power cars, since it is more valuable as food. But governments pay distillers to make alcohol from corn, so that corn prices will be higher and benefit the corporations that grow the corn.

But there are many non-food products that can be more cheaply grown than manufactured. Carnauba wax, candelilla wax, jojoba oil, gum arabic, gum tragacanth, and natural rubber are just a few.

In some cases, plants are most useful as sources of chemicals, such as in medicine and pest control. Because plants make many very complex molecules that are very hard to produce synthetically, many medicinal proteins and drugs come from plants. Roughly one-quarter of all prescription drugs are derived from plants.

Plant-derived insecticides and insect repellants are another class of molecule that is cheaper to get from plants than to try to make in a lab. These molecules also have the benefit of being easily biodegradable, so they don't linger in the environment.

Plant-derived dyes are another class of chemicals that are cheaper to grow than to make. *Carotenoids*—the red, yellow, and orange molecules in autumn leaves—are widely used in industry. Indigo blue, the browns of henna, and the yellows of saffron and turmeric are other examples.

Why do we use plants?

In addition to food, medicine, and industrial chemicals, we mostly use plant materials for their structural qualities.

Plants use four types of molecules to keep their shape and give strength to their cell walls. This strength is what holds up trees such as giant redwoods against gravity. The four molecules are lignin, cellulose, hemicellulose, and pectin, in order of how strong the molecules make the cell walls.

Lignin is a huge molecule, and it links together many other molecules. It is what makes wood a good structural material.

Cellulose is also a huge molecule, a *polymer*, made up of long chains of thousands of molecules of the simple sugar glucose.

Hemicellulose is made up of a number of different simple sugars all chained together. It is a more random molecule than cellulose—it doesn't crystallize, and has less strength.

Pectin is another large molecule made up of many different simple sugars all linked together. Pectins are why unripe fruits are hard. As the fruit ripens, the pectins break down, and the soft fruit can be eaten by animals that distribute the seeds for the plant.

Cellulose and lignin are the two most abundant organic polymers on earth. We use them together in wood products to build our houses and furniture and to make paper.

The lignin in newsprint paper is what makes the paper yellow with age. More expensive papers are made by removing almost all of the lignin, leaving mostly cellulose, which makes a nice white paper.

Cotton and flax are plant fibers used for making cloth and paper. Linen (made from flax fibers) is made of lignin and cellulose. Cotton is 95 percent cellulose.

Why are there so many colors of plants?

Plants have three main pigment molecules in their leaves. These are chlorophylls, carotenoids, and anthocyanins. Besides the leaves, plants may also have colorful bark.

Most leaves are various shades of green. This is due to the chlorophylls. The name chlorophyll comes from the Greek words *chloros* (green) and *phyllon* (leaf). There are six types of chlorophylls in plants. The two main chlorophylls are chlorophyll a and chlorophyll b.

Chlorophyll a absorbs purple and orange light the most. Chlorophyll b absorbs mostly blue and yellow. Neither one absorbs green, so the leaf looks green because that light is reflected to our eyes instead of being absorbed by the leaf.

Chlorophyll molecules have a ring shape at one end, with a magnesium atom in the center. If you boil a leaf in water, this magnesium atom gets replaced by a hydrogen atom, and the color changes from bright green to the dull color of overcooked broccoli.

Carotenes are the pigments that make the yellows and oranges of corn, squash, and carrots.

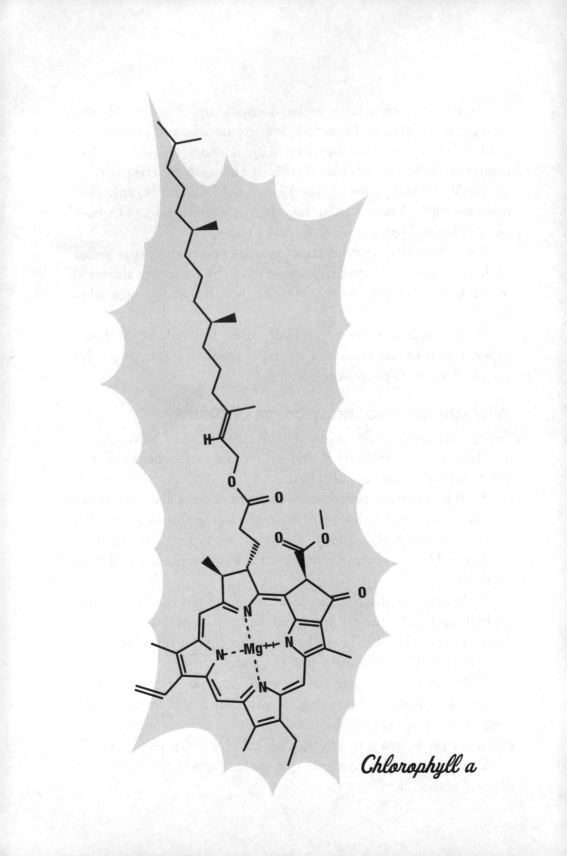

Chlorophyll a

Look how long the beta carotene molecule is. It has lots of double bonds (where you see two lines close together) alternating with single bonds (where there is only one line). These bonds between the carbons actually smear together, so that the electrons

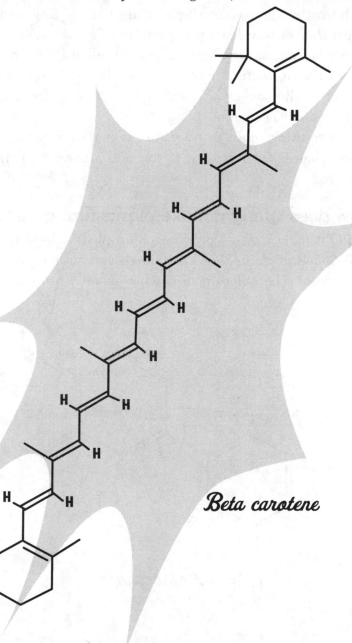

Beta carotene

slosh from one end of the molecule to the other, like water in a bathtub. The longer the molecule, the longer it takes to slosh to the other side. The sloshing electrons reflect light whose wavelength matches the sloshing—a long molecule reflects reds. Shorter groups of alternating double and single bonds, like the ring in chlorophyll, reflect shorter wavelengths of light, in this case green.

Anthocyanins are the third pigment plants use. They also have rings with alternating double and single bonds. They tend to be smaller, so they reflect blue and violet colors. Grape juice is purple because of anthocyanins.

A fun thing about anthocyanins is that they change their color if you change their acidity. If you add vinegar to grape juice, it turns red.

How does sunlight make plants turn green?

Sunlight makes plants produce chlorophyll. There is a lot more chlorophyll in plants than carotenoids and anthocyanins, so leaves look green. The chlorophyll is what absorbs sunlight to give the

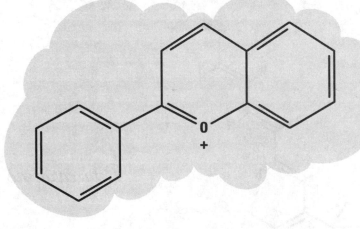

Anthocyanin

plant the energy it needs to make food out of water and the carbon dioxide in the air.

Chlorophyll is hard for a plant to make. A plant only makes it in places where it will do the most good (that is, collect the most sunlight). Most of the leaves are at the ends of branches and twigs and cast shadows on the rest of the plant, so the trunks of trees and the branches have little or no chlorophyll. The center leaves in cabbage, lettuce, and celery are also lighter in color because the plant does not waste precious chlorophyll on parts that get no sunlight.

If you look at a bean sprout, you will see that it is mostly white. That is partly because they are grown in the dark and don't get enough sunlight. The plant only produces chlorophyll when enough light hits it to make chlorophyll production worthwhile.

What makes leaves change colors?

Two things. One is the loss of chlorophyll, which removes the green pigment and allows the yellow carotenoid pigments to show. The other is the production of anthocyanins, which can be the blues and purples of flowers and fruits or the dark reds of autumn leaves.

Plants lose their leaves on purpose. When a leaf is damaged by wind or too much sun or when water and light are harder to come by, such as in a cold autumn, the plant will drop the leaf and either produce a new leaf or go dormant for the winter.

When a tree is about to lose a leaf, it stops sending nutrients to it and starts reclaiming some of the useful molecules in the leaf, to be stored or used elsewhere in the plant. Chlorophyll fades away and is not replaced. You can see the effects of this as a banana ripens. The green banana becomes yellow as the chlorophyll is lost and the yellow carotenoid pigments show through.

Anthocyanins are produced in some leaves as they prepare to fall. These pigments prevent damage from oxygen as the leaf is starved of nutrients, allowing time for the plant to absorb more useful molecules from the dying leaf. They also may be useful when they fall, since anthocyanins can prevent other plants from growing in the soil under the tree, leaving more resources for the tree in the spring.

Why are some plants glossy?

Plants that grow in dry areas and plants that don't lose their leaves in the fall have to protect themselves from drying out in hot summers and in winters when the water is frozen.

There are several tricks the plants can use to protect their leaves from drying out. One trick is to make the leaves into long, thin needles, so there is less surface to dry out. Pine trees use this trick.

Another trick is to curl the leaf up, like live oak leaves. This reduces water loss by reducing the wind and sun the leaf gets. Some leaves also have tiny hairs on them to reduce the water loss due to wind.

Yet another trick is to coat the leaves with a thick coat of protective wax, so the water stays trapped in the leaf. This protective coating of hard wax makes a glossy coat on the leaf, just like waxing a car.

What is herbicide?

An herbicide is a poison that kills plants. A weed-killer.

Many plants produce their own herbicides, so they can prevent other plants from using up their water, sunlight, or nutrients. The other plants can't grow underneath plants whose roots produce poisonous chemicals or whose leaves fall down and leak poisons into the soil.

The leaves of bay laurel trees produce natural herbicides that prevent other plants from growing up next to them. The flavor of bay leaves is in part due to these toxic (to plants) molecules. Walnut trees also produce natural herbicides.

Humans also make herbicides to control weeds. Some commercial herbicides kill almost any plant. Others are designed to only kill broad-leafed plants and not affect the grasses used for lawns. Some of those work by acting like growth hormones when they are absorbed by the leaves. Plants with broad leaves absorb so much they grow faster than they can get nutrients, and so they die. Grasses have narrower leaves, don't absorb as much, and only grow a little more than they normally would.

Herbicides like Roundup use a chemical called *glyphosate.* Glyphosate prevents a plant enzyme from producing three amino acids that are critical to the plant. Since most plants need to produce these amino acids, glyphosate is a wide-spectrum herbicide that kills most plants it is used on.

Selective herbicides are often synthetic molecules that mimic plant hormones. One selective herbicide is 2,4-D. It is inexpensive and kills broadleaf plants while leaving grasses mostly unaffected. 2,4-D mimics the plant hormone auxin. It is absorbed through the leaves of the plant and migrates to the fast growing parts of the plant, such as the tips of shoots. It stimulates the production in the plant of another hormone, ethylene, which can cause the leaves to fall off the plant if the dose is high enough.

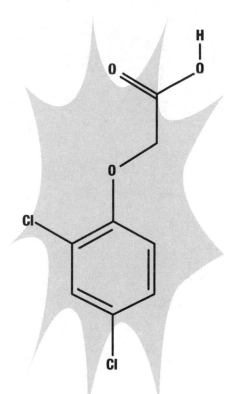

2,4-Dichlorophenoxyacetic acid (2,4-D)

3

Household Chemistry

What most people think of as chemicals are those things under the sink that are used to clean drains, polish silver, or disinfect kitchen counters. Those things with lots of long names in the ingredients list that are supposed to be kept out of reach.

But of course, everything that is made of atoms is a chemical. We use particular chemical reactions around the house to clean, bake, decorate, and glue. It is no surprise that most of Alexa's questions were about substances found in kitchen and bathroom cabinets.

How does soap work?

Oil and water don't normally mix. When you get grease or oil on your hands, it is not easy to wash it off with water alone.

This is because water molecules bind to each other much more strongly than they do to the oil. The water molecules stick together and leave the oil molecules behind. This is the same reason water and air don't mix. Water and sand don't mix because the sand molecules stick to one another better than they stick to water.

The surface between water and oil, or between water and air, is made up of water molecules that pull on one another. We call this pulling *surface tension*. If we can make the water molecules pull on each other a little less, we can relieve some of that surface tension. This would allow the water to spread out more if you spilled some, instead of beading up into little droplets. We say that water with less surface tension is wetter than normal water, because it can more easily make things wet.

Soap is a special kind of molecule. It has one end that is strongly attracted to water. But the rest of the molecule is an oil. Oils are long chains of carbon atoms with hydrogen atoms attached to them. There might be anywhere from 10 to 30 carbon atoms in the long chain.

The end of the soap molecule that is attracted to water sticks into the water at the surface. The rest of the long chain sticks out of the water, because the water doesn't stick to the oily parts of the chains.

Oil molecules don't pull on one another as strongly as water molecules do. The surface of the water now has a film of oily ends of soap molecules instead of water molecules. The surface tension is now much lower than it was, and the water doesn't bead up. It can reach into all the crevices of your hands or in between the fibers of clothes in the wash.

The soap forms the surface between the water and the air. But it also forms the surface between the water and any oil or grease on your hands. The long oily chains in the soap stick into the oil, and the water-loving ends stick into the water. As you scrub your hands together, you flatten any droplets of oil or water trapped between them. This lets more soap molecules form a surface between the oil and the water. When the water or the oil tries to form round droplets again, the bigger surface wrinkles and forms many tiny droplets instead of big ones.

The droplets don't get back together to form big droplets again, because there is a soap film between them. So as you scrub, the droplets get smaller and smaller. The tiny droplets, surrounded by soap molecules, no longer stick to your hands better than they do to the water. The water can now easily wash the tiny soap-coated oil droplets away.

Where does soap come from?

To make soap, take oil or fat and chemically add something that loves water to one end. Lye loves water. Lye is sodium hydroxide, a very powerful alkali. You can tell when a substance is strongly attracted to water because it releases heat when it reacts with water. When you add lye to water, the water gets very hot.

An *alkali* is the opposite of an acid. Acids and alkalis react strongly to produce salts. A fat or oil is three fatty acids attached to a molecule of glycerin. Adding lye to the fat allows the alkali to react with the fatty acids. The fatty acids are broken away from the glycerin and react with the lye to form soap. The glycerin is left behind.

The sodium part of the lye is now attached to the long chain of carbons that used to be a fatty acid. The sodium is still strongly attracted to water molecules, and the fatty acid end of the soap molecule ends up on the other side of the water surface, either in the air or in the oil.

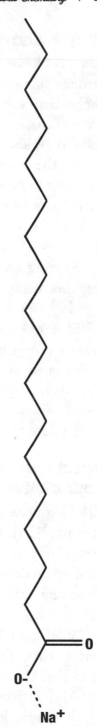

Sodium stearate – soap

Why is shaving cream foamy?

If air is blown into soapy water, the soap molecules will quickly arrange themselves so that the fatty end is in the air bubble and the sodium end stays in the water. The bubble rises and meets the layer of soap at the top surface of the water. This surface has all of the fatty ends of the soap sticking up into the air.

As the bubble rises up, there are now two soap surfaces, one with the fatty ends of the soap facing the air outside and another with its fatty ends facing the air inside the bubble. The sodium ends of the soap hold on to the very thin layer of water between the two soap film surfaces. This is what soap bubbles are made of.

Shaving cream used to be made by mixing soap and water together using a shaving brush. The many bristles of the brush acted like a whisk to make lots of tiny bubbles.

Shaving cream in a can is a mixture of oils and soaps combined with a propellant made from propane or butane gas. The gas is under pressure (so much pressure that the butane is a liquid in the can). When the user pushes the button on the can, the pressure forces out the soap, and the gas expands into bubbles. The tiny bubbles are so small and numerous that they form a stiff lather.

What chemicals in washing soap make it clean your clothes?

The chemicals that clean your clothes work a lot like ordinary soap (see page 25): they're made up of molecules that stick to oil or grease on one end and to water on the other end, allowing them to pick up dirt and grime and then be washed away. But unlike soap, these chemicals are specially formulated to avoid causing what we call soap scum.

Soap scum forms when soaps reacts with *hard water*, which is water that contains too much magnesium and calcium. Soap is a fatty acid chain with the acid end neutralized by sodium. Sodium has 11 electrons, and the one outer electron is only loosely held by the atom. Its other 10 electrons are held very tightly by the

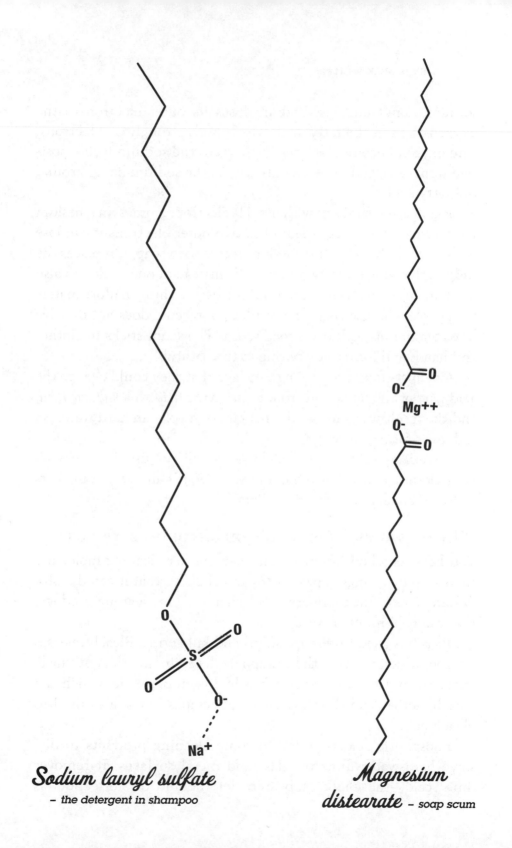

Sodium lauryl sulfate
– the detergent in shampoo

Magnesium distearate – soap scum

sodium atom's nucleus. Sodium loses its outer electron to the oxygen atom in the fatty acid, which pulls strongly on electrons. The oxygen becomes negatively charged, the sodium is left positively charged, and opposites attract, so the sodium hangs around the fatty acid.

Right after sodium with its 11 electrons comes magnesium with 12 electrons. Magnesium has two outer electrons it can lose to fatty acids. So when magnesium reacts with soap, it replaces the sodium, hanging on to two fatty acids instead of one. Calcium also has two outer electrons, and it does the same thing. Unfortunately for people who use soap, the resulting molecule does not dissolve in water and instead forms soap scum. The scum sticks to clothes and hands and forms a dirty ring in the bathtub.

Chemists found out a long time ago that they could change the acid part of the fatty acid from a *carboxylic acid* to a *sulfuric acid*, and the result was a molecule that could dissolve in hard water, so it doesn't form soap scum.

Molecules like these are called *detergents*. You use them to wash your clothes, and you use them to wash your hair. Even some bars of "soap" are actually detergent bars.

Why do we use chemicals as cleaning supplies?

You have seen how chemists can make better cleaning molecules than soap by changing part of the molecule so that it can dissolve in hard water. But there are other chemicals in cleaning products that can help in other ways.

Bleach is used to remove stains and kill germs. Bleach releases oxygen, which reacts with the stain or the germ. In effect, it slowly burns them. One kind of bleach is hydrogen peroxide, which can bleach clothes and disinfect cuts and scrapes but is also used to bleach hair.

Phosphoric acid is added to some cleaning products to dissolve hard-water films on glass and metal surfaces. It removes lime scale—the chalky substance left behind on coffeepots as

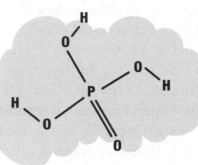

Phosphoric acid

*– cleans hard-water deposits
from glass*

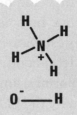

Ammonium hydroxide

– a strong alkali for cleaning glass

hard water is boiled—by dissolving the calcium and magnesium compounds that form it. Phosphoric acid is a strong acid, but in dilute form it is added to cola drinks to give them a tart taste. Acids taste sour.

Ammonium hydroxide is a strong alkali that reacts with fats and oils in much the same way lye does, forming water-soluble soap. It is used in glass cleaning products to remove grease and oils from windows.

Alcohols dissolve grease and fats, and one alcohol, isopropanol, is used to remove grease from skin and to disinfect the skin (it is sometimes called rubbing alcohol). It is added to window cleaners to help remove oils and grease.

How do they make shampoo in different colors?

The main detergents in most shampoos are sodium lauryl sulfate and sodium lauryl ether sulfate (sometimes called sodium laureth sulfate). These are white solids or powders in their pure form, and when dissolved in water they form a thick liquid that is very slightly off-white, like lemonade.

Shampoo manufacturers generally like prettier colors than that. They may add natural colors like tea extracts and plant dyes such as henna, beta carotene, and annatto, but these may require additional preservatives to keep them from spoiling during storage.

The Federal Food, Drug, and Cosmetic Act regulates food and cosmetic colorings, among other things. Some colors do not require certification by the FD&C because they are "Generally Recognized As Safe," or GRAS. These include such things as caramel color, beet juice, cochineal extract, saffron, mica, and beta carotene.

Unlike the colors that do not need to be certified, which contain a mixture of different compounds, each FD&C certified color is a pure compound. There are seven lists of colors. The first list is colors that are allowed in foods. The second list can be used in drugs and cosmetics. The third list is for only externally applied drugs and cosmetics. The other lists either exempt colors or add further restrictions.

The first list contains the FD&C colors. You may have seen these in the ingredients list on foods you have eaten.

- *FD&C Blue #1*
- *FD&C Blue #2*
- *FD&C Green #3*
- *FD&C Red #3*
- *FD&C Red #40*
- *FD&C Yellow #5*
- *FD&C Yellow #6*

The colors in the second list are not to be used in foods, and so the F is not included in the name. Some examples are:

- *D&C Green #5*
- *D&C Orange #5*
- *D&C Red #6*
- *D&C Red #7*
- *D&C Red #21*

- *D&C Red #22*
- *D&C Red #28*
- *D&C Red #30*
- *D&C Red #33*
- *D&C Red #36*
- *D&C Yellow #10*

Carmine (also known as cochineal extract) is one color that may surprise many people. It is made from the body and legs of a female scale insect that lives on cactus plants. Almost one-quarter of the dry weight of these insects is carminic acid, which the insects produce to prevent other insects from eating them. This is mixed with aluminum or calcium salts to make the red dye called carmine. You have probably eaten something colored with this dye, made from little tiny bugs.

Why is conditioner always white?

It isn't. It often is colored using the same colors that are used for shampoo. But before getting added colors, conditioner is white, and opaque. It is white and opaque for the same reason milk is white and opaque. Like milk, it has tiny droplets of oils and fats surrounded by water. These droplets scatter the light that hits it, just like the droplets of water in a cloud do. We see the result as opaque and white.

Hair conditioner has several ingredients in it that each do their own task to condition the hair. Hair has millions of tiny scales on each strand, and if these scales stand up away from the hair, it makes the hair tangle more easily and appear dull.

Acids, like citric acid, are added to conditioner because the acid makes the scales lie down against the hair.

Conditioner also has some detergents like shampoo does. But the detergents in conditioner are designed to stay in the hair. The water-loving end of the detergent sticks to the protein the hair is made of. The other end of the detergent is a long chain that sticks to oils and fats. This allows the detergent to hold on to the hair and the oil at the same time, so the oil coats the hair. This makes the hair shiny and helps prevent tangles.

One of the detergents used is *panthenol*, a precursor chemical to vitamin B_5 (pantothenic acid). It holds on to the hair protein and also holds on to water. Besides coating the hair and making it shiny, it also lubricates it to prevent tangles. It is sometimes called a *provitamin*, but it has no nutritive value when added to hair, which is just protein and has no living cells.

Other anti-tangle ingredients are silicone-based lubricants, such as dimethicone, and fatty alcohols (synthetic detergents made from oils). When you see stearyl alcohol or cetyl alcohol, those are fatty alcohols. Cetearyl alcohol is a mixture of the two. They help make the conditioner opaque, in addition to their lubricating and stabilizing functions.

How do they make shampoo and conditioner in fragrant smells?

Shampoo without any perfumes would smell like the detergents it is made of. This is not a particularly pleasant smell. Even "unscented" products usually include a *masking scent*, which is a perfume designed to hide the odor of the other ingredients without having a lingering effect in the hair.

Coming up with a good perfume scent for a shampoo involves overcoming several obstacles—cost, stability, safety, color—and optimizing for the desired characteristics—a unique scent, how well the hair holds the scent, how the shampoo smells in the bottle, or how long the scent lasts.

With over 3,000 perfume elements to choose from, the perfumer will choose the much smaller set of scents desired for the shampoo. For example, it turns out that more people like fruity-smelling shampoos than other scents. The chemist will then select from that list the scents that work well with the other ingredients in the shampoo. Some scents will be destroyed or changed by the detergent and can't be used. Other scents won't dissolve well in the

PROJECT:

PAPER CHROMATOGRAPHY

Materials

Food coloring (yellow, red, and green)
Paper towel
Jar
1 teaspoon salt
2 cups water
Wire coat hanger
Binder clip
¼ cup rubbing alcohol (optional)
¼ cup nail polish remover or acetone (optional)

Chemists have many ways to separate mixtures of compounds into their individual components. But few are as colorful and simple as paper chromatography.

You may have seen or even done paper chromatography, but this project goes into a little more detail than is usually seen in popular books and websites.

The photo on the next page shows four spots of food coloring on a strip of paper towel: yellow, red, and green, as well as a spot made of all three colors combined. The end of the paper is resting in a jar of 1 percent saltwater solution (1 teaspoon of salt in 2 cups of water). As the salt water wicks up into the towel, it carries some of the dye molecules faster than it does others. Pure water could be used, but the salt water helps make some compounds move faster up the paper than others.

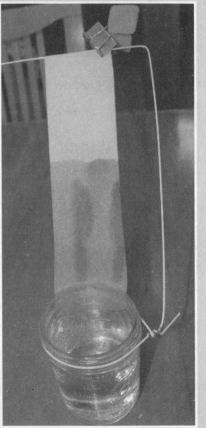

The entire setup is shown on the right. A bit of wire from a coat hanger and a binder clip support the paper towel, and you can see the colors have separated as they climbed up the paper.

On the next page, the different areas are marked with labels. The box of food coloring that was used says it contains the colors FD&C Yellow #5, FD&C Blue #1, FD&C Red #40, and FD&C Red #3. Notice that there is no green color listed, and there are two different colors of red.

The two reds show up as separate areas of color. The bottom one is a slightly magenta red, and the upper one is a slightly orange red. Combined, they make the color that the dye manufacturer wanted, a rich solid red color.

The green food coloring has also separated into two patches of color. The blue color climbed the towel quickly, staying with the very top of the water that wicked up into the towel. Below it is a patch of yellow, still stained faintly with some of the blue, so it appears a little greener than the pure yellow in the first column.

FD&C Blue #1
Rf = 1.0

FD&C Yellow #5
Rf = 0.83

Rf = 0.56
FD&C Red #40

In the last column, three of the four colors have separated. The yellow and one of the reds seem to climb the paper at the same rate, and stay mixed. But the blue raced to the top, and the magenta red lagged behind, barely moving.

The speed of the molecules relative to the salt water is called the *retardation factor*, or Rf. It is simply the distance the color has moved up the towel divided by the distance the water has moved. We use an estimate of where the center of the color spot is for the calculation.

The paper is called the *stationary phase* because it stays in place. The salt water is called the *mobile phase* because it is the part that climbs up the towel. The colors are called the *analyte* because they are what we are analyzing.

Paper chromatography separates compounds based on how polar they are. A *polar* molecule has one end that is more positively charged than the other end. A nonpolar molecule does not have charged ends. Paper is made of cellulose, which is a polar molecule. Salt water is also polar, but to a different extent. As the dye molecules encounter the paper and the salt water, some are bound more tightly to the paper, and some more tightly to the water. This causes the separation.

You can take advantage of this effect by using solvents that are less polar than water—for instance, isopropyl alcohol (rubbing alcohol) or acetone (nail polish remover)—to get different separations. ***With adult supervision***, you can experiment with ¼ cup of each one to see what works best for the molecules you are trying to separate.

Using 91 percent isopropyl alcohol, the following chromatogram shows that Red #3 travels faster than the others.

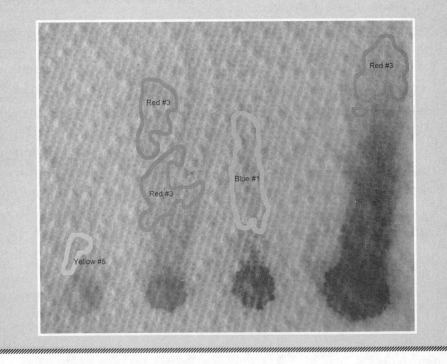

The other colors don't separate nearly as well as they did in water. In acetone (not shown), only the Red #3 moved. What this shows us is that Red #3 is the least polar of the molecules, and Blue #1 is the most polar.

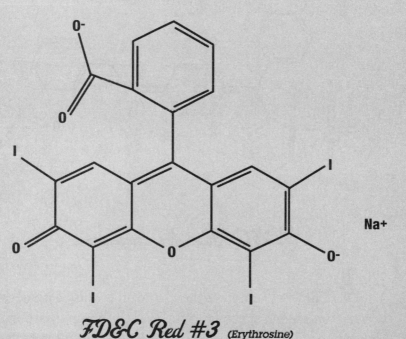

FD&C Red #3 (Erythrosine)

Red #3, shown above, is not very polar. Both ends have negative oxygen atoms attracting positive sodium atoms.

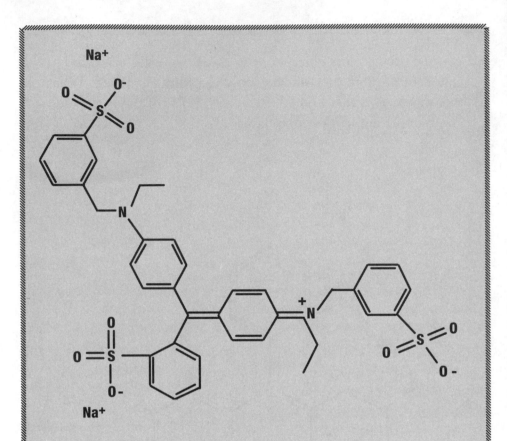

FD&C Blue #1 (Brilliant Blue)

FD&C Blue #1, on the other hand, has one of its negative oxygen atoms alone at the far right, and the compensating positive nitrogen atom is buried towards the middle. This molecule is more polar than the other colors.

Red #40 and Yellow #5 are very similar molecules. That is why they are hard to separate. They react similarly to both the paper and the solvent.

While chromatography was originally invented to separate colored molecules, the technique is so useful that it is now

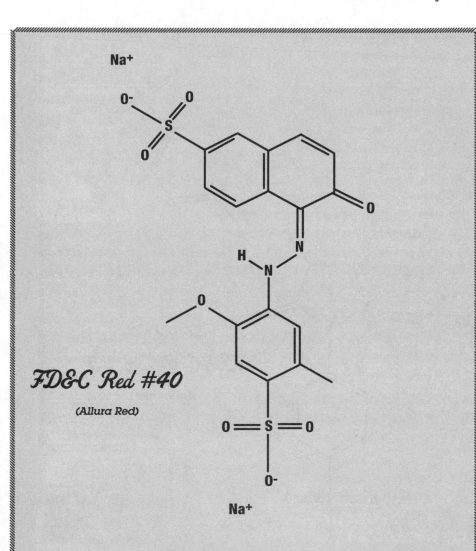

FD&C Red #40

(Allura Red)

used for a large number of molecules that have no color. To make them visible, chemists can view them in ultraviolet light and look for fluorescence, or they can add a chemical to the developed chromatogram that makes the different spots visible. One such chemical is iodine. Vapors of iodine are allowed to react with the finished chromatogram, and the resulting compounds are often colored.

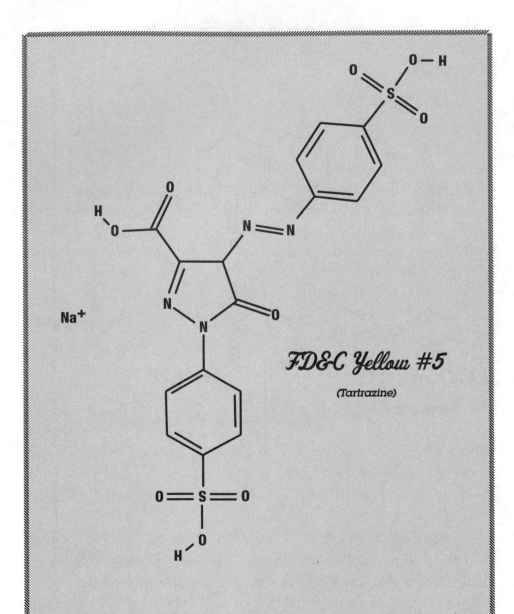

FD&C Yellow #5

(Tartrazine)

Other types of chromatography use sensors other than the human eye to distinguish the different molecules. This allows scientists to analyze a huge number of molecules that do not interact with visible light.

shampoo, or they won't release from the shampoo well enough to be detected. Some of them will stick to the hair well, and others won't.

Many perfumes are made of *essential oils*. Here the word *essential* does not mean that you can't do without it but instead refers to the fact that the oil was extracted from a flower, fruit, or some other thing as an essence. This is often done by heating the material until it boils and then collecting and condensing the vapors (distilling). Other methods are solvent extraction, where the material is crushed in a solvent such as alcohol to dissolve the oils, and chromatography, where the oils wick up in a substance and separate out according to how fast they travel.

There may be 300 different compounds in an essential oil. Usually the compounds include one or more molecules that give it its characteristic odor. These molecules can be used by themselves instead of the essential oil to reduce cost or ensure reproducibility and stability in the final product.

Some examples of molecules that have characteristic scents are shown below.

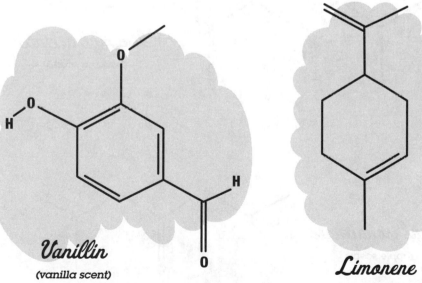

Vanillin
(vanilla scent)

Limonene
(citrus scent)

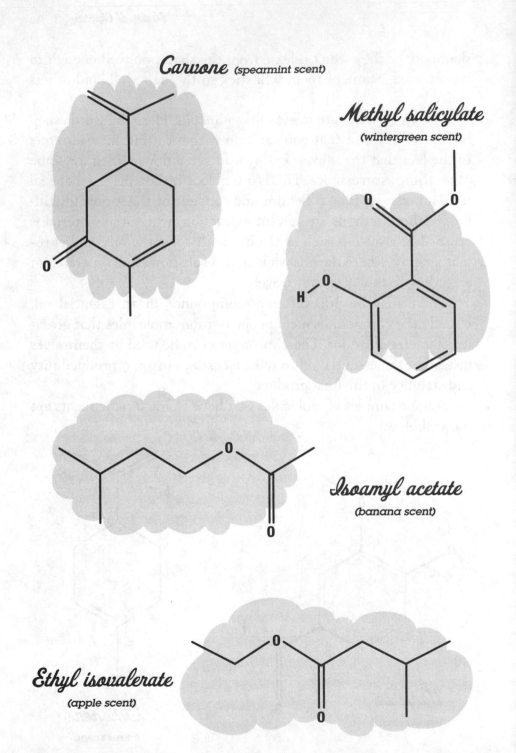

Carvone (spearmint scent)

Methyl salicylate
(wintergreen scent)

Isoamyl acetate
(banana scent)

Ethyl isovalerate
(apple scent)

What does glass have to do with chemistry?

Glassware is used a lot in chemistry. It is transparent, so you can watch the reactions happen. It is fairly easy to clean. It resists heating, so you can hold it over a flame to speed up a reaction or distill off a solvent. And it is fairly inexpensive.

Glass is usually made from silica (silicon dioxide, what you probably know as sand or quartz), with some sodium oxide and calcium oxide added, along with some other minor ingredients. This kind of glass is called soda-lime glass and is easy to melt and cheap.

Chemists often use borosilicate glass, which is mostly silica with some sodium oxide, aluminum oxide, and boric oxide. It resists heat shock (when something breaks if you heat it), and so it is used for heating things. Another type of glass that is good for this is fused silica, which is just pure quartz, heated to very high temperatures until it melts and can be formed. It is expensive because of the high heat required to make it.

Glass can be colored by adding other compounds, such as metal oxides. Nickel oxide makes yellows and purples, cobalt oxide gives a rich blue, and gold and copper make reds.

Lead glass is like soda-lime glass, but lead oxide is substituted for the calcium oxide and some of the silica. Since lead is so heavy, the resulting glass might be one-quarter lead by weight. Adding the lead oxide makes the glass bend light more than other glasses do, which adds sparkle to cut glass and chandelier ornaments. It is sometimes called lead crystal because of the cut shapes, but glass is not a crystal—the molecules in any glass are all in random order, like they are in a liquid.

That disordered state is characteristic of glasses. Silica by itself would tend to crystallize, like a quartz crystal. Adding sodium oxide and calcium or magnesium oxide makes the molecules much more complex, forming networks that are too disordered to crystallize.

PROJECT:

SILICON BOUNCY BALL

Materials

2 tablespoons sodium silicate solution (available at drugstores)
1 tablespoon rubbing alcohol
Disposable cup
Wooden craft stick or disposable plastic spoon
Warm, running water

Adult supervision required

Sodium silicate, also known as water glass or egg keep, is made by reacting quartz with molten sodium carbonate. That is not exactly an easy or safe thing to do at home, however. Another way to make it is to add silica gel (the sandy stuff in those little packets that keep shoe boxes and other packages dry) to a hot solution of lye (sodium hydroxide in water). This is also not exactly a safe thing to play with at home. So it is a good thing that sodium silicate solution is sold in drugstores (although usually behind the counter where you have to ask for it), because sodium silicate is fun to play with.

Sodium silicate got the name *egg keep* from the practice of coating eggs with it to preserve them before refrigeration was common. It seals the pores in the egg's shell so that no oxygen can get in. It is also a fireproofing treatment for wood, paper, and cloth for the same reason: oxygen can't get to the flammable materials.

Those little packets of silica gel mentioned earlier? They are made from sodium silicate. Manufacturers add a little acid,

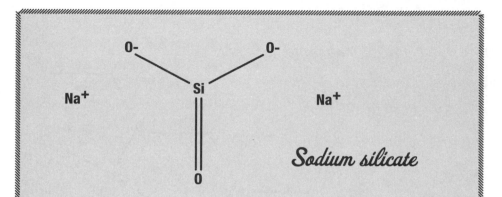

such as hydrochloric acid or even vinegar, to the water glass to make a firm gel. When they dry that gel out in an oven, the water is driven off, and what remains is a delicate network of silicate crystal that has an amazingly large surface area (800 square meters per gram). At the same time the surface attracts water from the air. The result is a very good material to put in packages to protect parts from moist air.

You may have seen "magic garden" kits in toy stores or gift shops. You drop little rocks into a special solution, and the rocks slowly grow into colorful stalagmites that look like little rock trees. The solution they grow in is sodium silicate. The little rocks are made from colorful salts of metals such as copper, cobalt, and manganese.

The bits of copper sulfate or cobalt chloride dissolve and start to react with the sodium silicate, forming insoluble silicate shells around the soluble sulfates or chlorides. But the silicate shells still allow water to get to the crystals inside, and the result is cracks caused by the expansion. The salt solution squirts out, and a new insoluble silicate layer forms around it. This process repeats, forming towers and branches, each with the color of the original salt.

In this project, you are going to use sodium silicate to make a super bouncy ball.

Polydiisopropyl silicate

Silicon is right below carbon in the periodic table of the elements, and like carbon, silicon can form polymers (long chains of molecules). You may have used silicone rubber as a glue or sealant. You can make the sodium silicate solution polymerize into long chains by adding an alcohol, such as ethanol or the isopropanol (rubbing alcohol) in your medicine cabinet. The result is polydiethyl or polydiisopropyl silicate.

Place 2 tablespoons of sodium silicate solution into a disposable cup, and add 1 tablespoon of rubbing alcohol.

Next, stir the mixture with a craft stick or disposable plastic spoon for a few seconds to get a thick white mass of

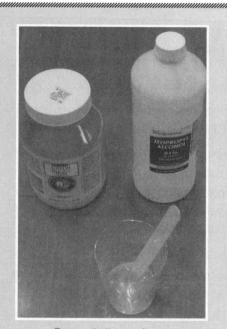

Bouncy ball ingredients

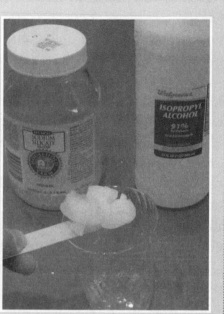

Bouncy ball mixing complete

polymerized polydiisopropyl silicate, mixed with some water and alcohol.

Now form the mass into a ball with your hands, under running warm water. The warm water helps remove the excess alcohol and form the ball more easily. It also helps wash the slimy polymer from your hands.

The result of our two-minute effort is a remarkably bouncy ball. If dropped, it recovers a large part of the height of the drop on each bounce.

Completed polydiisopropyl silicate bouncy ball

What is toothpaste made from?

It is not a paste made from teeth. Toothpaste is made from abrasives and detergents, usually with other minor ingredients to add special features.

A simple toothpaste can be made from baking soda and salt. Both of these ingredients act as abrasives to help the toothbrush scrub off the film in the mouth left by germs.

About half of a typical toothpaste is abrasives. Typical abrasives used are sodium bicarbonate (baking soda), calcium carbonate (chalk), aluminum hydroxide, hydroxyapatite, and hydrated silica (opal). Hydroxyapatite is as hard as tooth enamel, and hydrated silica is harder than tooth enamel, so both of those can wear the teeth down more than the softer abrasives listed before them.

The detergents used in toothpaste are generally the same ones used in shampoo. They help clean your teeth in the same way as shampoo cleans your hair, and they create the foam when you brush. You can't taste the detergent because toothpastes are usually very strongly flavored to overcome the taste of what the brush is removing from the teeth.

Tooth enamel can be strengthened against cavities by adding fluoride to toothpaste. Antibacterial agents are sometimes added to kill bacteria that form films of plaque. Sodium polyphosphate is added to toothpaste to reduce the formation of tartar—plaque that has become hardened by the calcium phosphate salts in saliva. Whitening toothpastes contain peroxides that bleach the teeth.

What are shoes made from?

Dress shoes are still mostly made of leather. Athletic shoes these days are mostly rubber, plastic, and cloth, sometimes with a little leather.

Untreated animal skins absorb water and rot easily. To prevent this, the skins are tanned. Tanning is a process in which skins are treated with chemicals that cause the proteins to link together, called *cross-linking*. Tanning makes the leather more waterproof, less likely to rot, and more supple.

Tanning is a complex operation, involving steps to remove fats and hair from the skins, adjusting the acidity of the skins, and then allowing the skins to soak in a tanning solution. The tanning solution can use *tannins*, a kind of acid found in oak bark and other plant tissue, or it can use chromium compounds, which tan the hide faster and make a leather that is more resistant to shrinkage.

The soles of shoes can be made of leather but are increasingly made from synthetic materials that offer better traction, durability, and water resistance. Some of the materials used are ethylene vinyl acetate, rubber, thermoplastic rubber, rubber foam, and polyurethane.

Thermoplastic rubber is actually two compounds mixed together. One is styrene, the plastic that model airplanes are made out of. The other is a synthetic rubber called butadiene. The word *thermoplastic* means that the material can be melted and poured into molds, making it easy to form shoe soles with traction patterns in them. It also means they can be recycled.

Ethylene vinyl acetate is also a mix of two *polymers*. It is what hot glue sticks are made of. It is also what many foam rubber items are made from.

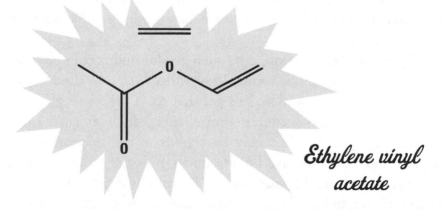

Ethylene vinyl acetate

The molecules shown on this page are the *monomers* of the plastic. These monomers are the molecules that link together into long chains to form the polymers that give the plastic its solid form, its rubbery texture, and other qualities.

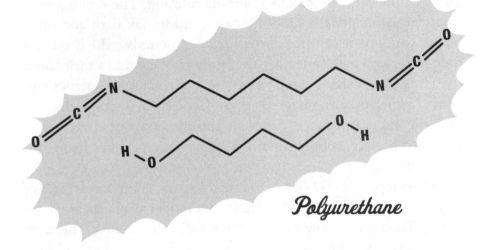

Polyurethane

What is in deodorant?

Perfumes in deodorant mask odors. Moisturizers make the skin feel soft and make the product glide onto the skin. Oils are added to make the deodorant more transparent so that it hides better on skin and clothing. Silica is added to absorb skin oils that accumulate from sweat.

To control perspiration, salts such as aluminum chlorohydrate or aluminum zirconium tetrachlorohydrex GLY are used. These dissolve in the sweat and make a gel that coats the sweat glands.

Aerosol deodorants contain propellants, which are gases under atmospheric pressure but may be liquids in the deodorant can. Butane and isobutane are liquids under pressure or at temperatures you can reach in your freezer. Propane is a gas in the can or in the freezer and is added to the butane to get a higher pressure.

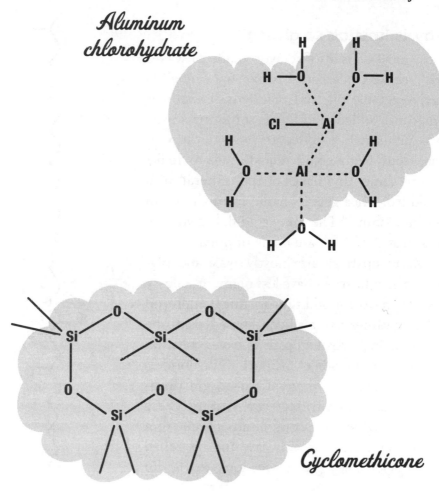

Aluminum chlorohydrate

Cyclomethicone

The mix of gases is tailored to the exact pressure needed to propel the other ingredients out of the can without spraying too hard.

In addition to the propellant, a carrier fluid is used to carry the ingredients out in the spray. Cyclomethicone is one common carrier fluid used in aerosol deoderants.

Roll-on deodorants usually have water and alcohol to dissolve the ingredients. The alcohol gives a cooling effect as it dries.

In solid antiperspirants, the ingredients are blended into a solid carrier, which might be a hydrogenated oil or a fatty alcohol like stearyl alcohol.

Why is lipstick so glossy?

Mica. Lipstick is a soft crayon made of waxes like beeswax, carnauba wax, or candelilla wax, vegetable oil, and pigments. Lanolin is sometimes added, and talc is sometimes used also. Vitamin E is added to protect the vegetable oils from going rancid. But to make the lips shine, tiny flakes of the mineral mica are added. Mica gets its name from the Latin word for "shine." The shiny gold flakes you see in sand at the beach are made of mica.

Matte lipsticks are mostly wax and pigment. Sheer lipsticks have less pigment. Glossy lipsticks have (in addition to mica) more oil and sometimes use a silicone-based oil to be longer lasting. Frosted lipsticks have a pearlizing compound made of bismuth oxychloride.

Other glossy compounds used are diisostearyl malate and triisostearyl citrate. These are *esters*, which are compounds made from alcohols and acids, in this case the fat called stearic acid. They give a wet look to the lip gloss.

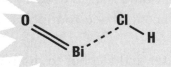

Bismuth oxychloride

Diisostearyl malate

How do people make lipstick different colors?

Most lipstick pigments are shades of red. The most popular red pigment used in lipsticks is carmine, a dye made from the shell of a tiny scale insect that lives on cactus in the US Southwest.

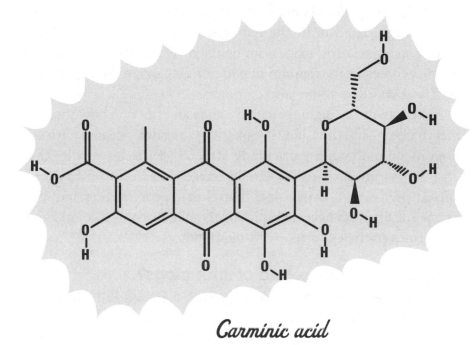

Carminic acid

The dye itself is carminic acid, which is used in many foods and cosmetics. It is sometimes called cochineal extract. Only the female insect has the dye—a natural defense to keep other insects from eating the little critters. They sit on the cactus with their little straws sipping cactus juice, looking like little scales (which is why they are called scale insects). They can't run away, so they make carminic acid, which other bugs don't like.

Cochineal extract is also used in fruit juices like ruby red grapefruit juice, strawberry orange juice, pomegranate cherry juice, and many others. Like any other natural color derived from living things, cochineal extract usually contains some proteins from the original source, and some people have allergic reactions to the proteins. For this reason, and because some people don't like the idea of eating bugs, some manufacturers are moving to synthetic dyes like FD&C Red #40. But that dye has a slightly more orange color.

Other red pigments used in lipsticks are made from iron compounds. In other words, the red comes from rust. Both red iron oxides and black iron oxides can be used. White pigment for pink lipstick comes from titanium dioxide or zinc oxide. Synthetic dyes such as D&C Red #6 are also common.

The size of the pigment particles has an effect on how the light hits the eye—and thus, how it looks. Mica particles coated with colored metal oxides are particularly affected. Particles smaller than 25 microns produce a silky effect. Larger sizes up to 50 microns appear pearlescent. Larger sizes than that appear brighter and sparkly. Some lipsticks have metallic silver, gold, or copper colors made from mica particles coated with pigments.

How does Drano get rid of sink clogs?

Drano is made of lye (sodium hydroxide), mixed with little bits of aluminum metal. When lye crystals mix with water, they react strongly and produce a lot of heat. The hot water softens lumps of grease in the drain. The sodium hydroxide then reacts with the softened grease, turning it into soap. The bits of aluminum metal also react with the sodium hydroxide, releasing more heat but also releasing a lot of hydrogen gas, which makes bubbles that further loosen the fat and grease in the clog.

The hot water dissolves the soap. The bubbles of hydrogen break up the lumps of grease and make them float up away from the clog, so more hot water and lye can react with the grease and fat.

If there is hair in a clog, the lye also dissolves that, and the hydrogen bubbles loosen the strands from one another, so that the clog catches more water and is carried down the drain.

So there are many chemical reactions going on at once. Heating the water, making soap, making bubbles, and dissolving proteins. Add to this the force of new water pushing on what remains of the clog, and lye-based drain cleaners do a pretty good job.

Lye can cause burns to skin and eyes, so caution should be used with any product that contains sodium hydroxide.

How does hairspray get out of the can?

Hairsprays use propellants. A *propellant* is a gas or a liquid under pressure. When the pressure is released, the liquid boils or the gas expands, carrying with it any other ingredients in the can. In the case of hairspray, those ingredients are the polymers (basically glue) that hold the hair in place.

But propellants are used to get other things out of spray cans as well. And the contents of the can dictate which propellant is used.

For example, hairspray uses propane, butane, and isobutane as propellants, because the polymers in the spray dissolve easily in butane, which is a liquid under the kind of pressures in the can. Propane also dissolves in butane, so less pressure is needed to contain a lot of propane in the can. The mix of the three propellants is adjusted so that the spray comes out at just the right pressure. Too much propane, and the spray comes out too hard. Too little, and there is not enough force to carry the ingredients to your hair.

Some hairsprays use dimethyl ether or methyl ethyl ether as propellants. These are similar in function to butane, and like butane, are flammable.

The propellant in whipped cream is nitrous oxide (laughing gas). This gas dissolves easily in fats and is also used for cooking sprays. Using a gas that dissolves in the other ingredients in the can allows a lot of gas to be put into the can without using a lot of pressure. When you release the pressure on a can of whipped cream, the cream expands to four times its size in the can. But if air was used, the cream would only whip to half that volume. Air would also allow the cream to go rancid, since it has oxygen in it. Carbon dioxide would dissolve in the water in the cream, but then it would make carbonic acid, which would curdle the proteins in the cream.

Other propellants are pure nitrogen (it doesn't react with ingredients, but it doesn't dissolve well, so higher pressures are needed), and hydrofluorocarbons (they liquefy easily, they are non-flammable, they don't create smog, and the new ones are safe for the ozone layer).

How does superglue work?

Superglue is made from a small molecule called *ethyl cyanoacrylate*.

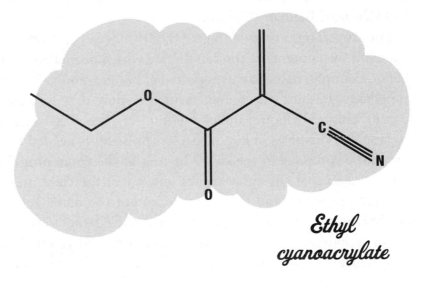

Ethyl cyanoacrylate

When these small molecules contact water, even the only very slightly dampness of dry fingers or wood, they quickly join up into long chains (polymers) that bond surfaces (such as fingers) together.

Superglue forms a strong bond with wood, plastic, and leather. It is used to lock nuts onto bolts because while it bonds well to metal, it has a low *shear strength*, so the nut can later be removed from the bolt using a wrench.

Formulations of superglue have been made for medical use, to glue wounds together without stitches and to slow bleeding.

Cyanoacrylates react strongly with cotton, generating heat and smoke, and can in some cases cause the cotton to ignite. They also react strongly with baking soda (sodium bicarbonate). This is some-times useful—for example, filling a hole with baking soda and then adding superglue can make a strong space-filling material.

How does hair dye work?

Hair can be dyed using simple coloring agents, such as henna, that simply add a dye or pigment to the hair, or it can be dyed using complicated chemical reactions that open up the hair shaft, bleach the hair to a lighter color, and then react with the hair to form a permanent bond that colors the hair the desired shade.

It is not easy to make a dye stay stuck to hair. This is a good thing if you want to dye your hair blue for Halloween. Temporary dyes usually have large molecules that cannot penetrate into the hair shaft. They will wash out easily with shampoo. Since they contain no bleaches or ammonia, they are gentle on hair.

If you want to cover gray or darken light hair, slightly more permanent dyes that will last a number of washings are available. Some don't use alkaline developers to open up the hair to absorb the dye; instead they rely on the small size of the dye molecules to help penetrate into the hair. They will last through four to five shampooings.

For a little more permanence (20 or more shampooings), a gentle alkali-like sodium carbonate and a low-strength solution of hydrogen peroxide can open up the hair and chemically bind the dye to the hair. Since the low strength of the peroxide does not bleach the hair, the resulting dye looks more natural, as the varia-tions in the hair still show through.

For the most permanent dye, one that will not wash out, ammonia and strong hydrogen peroxide are used. The peroxide bleaches the hair so that dark hair can be dyed a lighter color. But the main reason for using the peroxide is because the dye is actually formed from small molecules that bind to the hair and then react with the ammonia and peroxide to form larger molecules that are locked into the hair strand.

What is ammonia and how does it work?

There are two molecules that go by the common name *ammonia*. This first is a gas, made from a nitrogen atom and three hydrogen atoms.

Ammonia gas is also known as *anhydrous ammonia*, which means ammonia without water. Ammonia reacts with water in the environment very easily, so almost all of the ammonia you will ever encounter is actually ammonium hydroxide.

The ammonia molecule steals a hydrogen nucleus (a proton) from water. This makes the ammonium ion NH_4^+ and leaves the hydroxyl ion OH^- as the only thing left of the water molecule. Since they have opposite charges, they attract each other and hang

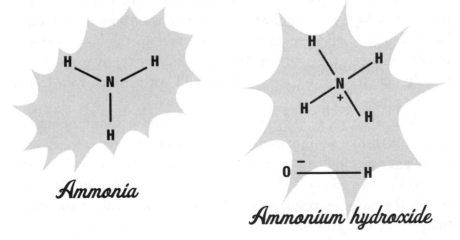

Ammonia

Ammonium hydroxide

around the same neighborhood. Household ammonia, used as a cleaning agent, is actually water and ammonium hydroxide.

Ammonia is a base, like lye (sodium hydroxide). Like lye, it can react with oils and fats to form soaps. As a cleaner, ammonia turns fats and oils on glass or tile surfaces into soap, and the water in the ammonia solution dissolves the soaps so the sponge or paper towel can carry them away. What is left is a solution of ammonium hydroxide, which then completely evaporates, leaving no streaks on the surface.

Animals make ammonia from proteins in the food they eat, and they use the ammonia to neutralize acids in their urine. This is why a crowded barn or stable has a strong ammonia scent.

What is antifreeze?

Antifreeze is anything that prevents water from freezing when the temperature drops below the freezing point. It works by lowering the freezing point of water.

The *freezing point* is the temperature at which water freezes as fast as it melts. Below the freezing point, molecules of water move slower and will be captured by the ice. Above the freezing point, ice will melt as the molecules of water move faster.

Because heat is the random motion of molecules, there will always be some water molecules that are moving fast enough to be liquid and some that are moving slow enough to be solid ice, no matter what the temperature. But if the temperature is too warm or too cold, you may not notice, since only a tiny amount will be in the "wrong" form and only for a tiny amount of time.

The balance between melting and freezing is easy to upset. If salt is added to ice, the salt will dissolve in the water on the surface of the ice. The salt molecules (or ions) mix with the water. So now, if the liquid part is half salt molecules and half water molecules, only half as many water molecules will hit the ice as they jostle around. This means the freezing rate will be half what it used to be. But the melting rate is unchanged, so the ice melts. The balance between freezing and melting has been upset.

To get the balance back, the temperature has to be lowered. This is why salt water freezes at a lower temperature than fresh water. Salt is thus an antifreeze.

Alcohol will do the same thing as salt. The alcohol molecules mix with the water, so fewer water molecules hit the ice. Alcohol is also an antifreeze. It is more expensive than salt, but it does not cause metals to corrode like salt does, so it is a better choice for use in a car.

An even better antifreeze than alcohol is *ethylene glycol*. If half the water is replaced with alcohol, the freezing point is lowered by 32° Celsius (57° Fahrenheit). If half the volume is ethylene glycol, the freezing point is lowered by 34° Celsius (62° Fahrenheit). This small improvement in freezing point is not as important as two other features of ethylene glycol: it is not as flammable as alcohol and it raises the boiling point of water.

Why do you need antifreeze in your car?

If you live in a place where the temperature never drops below freezing, you don't need antifreeze. But, as mentioned in the last answer, the antifreeze ethylene glycol also raises the boiling point of water, so you might still want to add it to your radiator water so

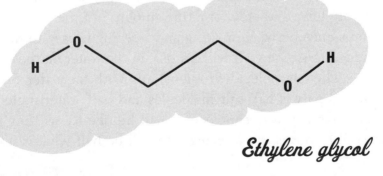

Ethylene glycol

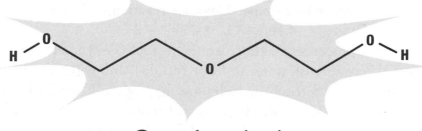

Diethylene glycol

the car doesn't boil over as easily as it would with water or a combination of alcohol and water.

Commercial antifreeze also contains rust inhibitors—silicates, phosphates, and borates—to make the engine last longer. These control corrosion by keeping the liquid slightly alkaline. A green or red dye is also added so you can tell antifreeze from other liquids that might leak under your car. Orange-dyed antifreeze has rust inhibitors made from organic acids, which last longer.

Another antifreeze ingredient is diethylene glycol, although usually it is found in much smaller amounts and sometimes only because it is an unwanted byproduct of ethylene glycol production.

Why does salt water make metal rust faster?

If you had pure iron and put it into pure water, very little would happen, since there would be no oxygen to react with the iron. And if you put the pure iron into pure dry oxygen, very little would also happen. The outer iron atoms would rust, but then that layer of rust would stand between the iron and the remaining oxygen.

Water helps iron react with oxygen. The first step in getting oxygen to react with iron is to break up the oxygen molecule. In water, oxygen can steal some electrons from iron to make four hydroxyl ions (the OH$^-$ ions in the following reaction):

$$O_2 + 4 \text{ e}^- + 2 \text{ H}_2O \rightarrow 4 \text{ OH}^-$$

The electrons come from the iron:

$$Fe \rightarrow Fe^{2+} + 2 \text{ e}^-$$

But to make rust we need another reaction with iron:

$$4 \, Fe^{2+} + O_2 \rightarrow 4 \, Fe^{3+} + 2 \, O_2^-$$

In the process of making rust, the ferrous (Fe^{2+}) and ferric (Fe^{3+}) ions also react with water to form $Fe(OH)_2$ and $Fe(OH)_3$ (ferrous hydroxide and ferric hydroxide) and hydrogen. These hydroxides can then lose their water to form still more iron compounds. It is all these reactions that end up making the rust flaky, so it falls off the iron and exposes new iron that can start to rust.

All of these reactions are sped up by acids and by having more ions in the water, so it conducts electricity better, so that the iron and oxygen can exchange electrons. Adding salt to the water makes the iron corrode more quickly, but adding an acid makes it corrode even faster than that.

How do water filters work?

Simple water filters just block large particles and let tiny water molecules go on through. You can see this effect when you rinse vegetables in a strainer or colander. The vegetables are the large "particles" that are blocked.

A paper towel will block smaller particles. You can use paper as a coffee filter, to keep the coffee grounds in the paper while the water and other small molecules (the ones that give coffee its flavor and color) go on through.

If you want to get rid of those other small molecules, you might use an activated charcoal filter. Charcoal is very good at absorbing small molecules that color and flavor water. This action is not actually filtering; it is absorbing.

Once the charcoal has absorbed a lot of those small molecules, it gets full and can't absorb any more. To reactivate it, you just heat it up. The small molecules boil off, and the charcoal is ready to absorb more again.

Paper filters and charcoal filters won't block tiny things like bacteria. For that, the holes in the filter must be very tiny. But that means that the filter has to be very big, because even the tiny water molecules will be blocked most of the time. An alternative is to use a lot of pressure to force the water through the filter.

One type of filter that uses a lot of pressure to force water through tiny pores is a *reverse osmosis* filter. In normal osmosis, a filter sits between pure water and salt water. The water can go through the filter in either direction, but the salt ions are too big to go through the filter. This means that more molecules end up on the salt side of the filter. To reverse this, a large pressure is used on the salt side of the filter to force the pure water through. So instead of water going from the pure side to the salty side, the direction is reversed, and you get pure water out.

How do water softeners work, and why do you need them?

In the discussion of how washing soap works (page 28), you learned how calcium and magnesium could attach to two soap molecules, making a large molecule that was too big to stay dissolved in the water. This large molecule is what forms soap scum, and it sticks to skin, hair, and fabric, gluing dirt onto them.

To make it easier for soap to work, calcium and magnesium ions are removed from the water. One way to do this is to add a chemical to the water that combines with the calcium and magnesium and makes them unavailable to combine with the soap. Citric acid will do this. So will sodium carbonate, which is why it is called *washing soda*.

Another way to remove the calcium and magnesium ions is to use a water softener. A water softener runs the water through a tank full of tiny plastic beads. These beads have a negative charge and collect positive ions.

At first the beads have sodium ions around them. But sodium ions only have a charge of +1. Calcium and magnesium have charges of +2, so they are attracted to the negatively charged plastic beads more than the sodium ions are. The two types of ions then exchange places. That is why the plastic the beads are made of is called an *ion exchange resin.*

At some point all of the sodium ions have been exchanged for calcium and magnesium ions, and the plastic beads have to be recharged with sodium ions. To do that, the water softener gives them an overwhelming supply of sodium ions by bathing them in very salty water. Even though the calcium and magnesium ions are more positive, there are so many sodium ions that the reaction goes into reverse.

Once the plastic beads are again coated with sodium ions, the salty water, which now has lots of calcium and magnesium ions in it, is flushed away, and the water-softening cycle repeats.

What chemicals does hairspray have?

Glue. Actually, vinyl acetate—what common white glue is made of—is one of the common ingredients, but other ingredients are in hairspray to modify the glue to be just right for holding hair.

Hairspray needs to start out as a bunch of tiny droplets of glue that run down strands of hair until they come to the place where two strands cross. The drop stops there and dries into a thin film of glue that holds the two strands together. Repeat this a few thousand times, and your hair will stay in place all day.

But hairspray also has to be a glue that washes out of your hair easily when you shampoo and can't remain sticky or become sticky on a humid day or in rain or fog. So usually a second polymer is added, one that is not water soluble. Hairspray is thus made of *copolymers,* which just means two kinds of glue.

The second polymer is often crotonic acid or vinylpyrrolidone.

The polymers are dissolved in alcohol and a solvent propellant such as butane or dimethyl ether.

Plasticizers make the glue more flexible. These might be silicones or fatty acid esters (fatty acids bound to alcohols) such as triethyl citrate. There are also usually some additives that are mainly

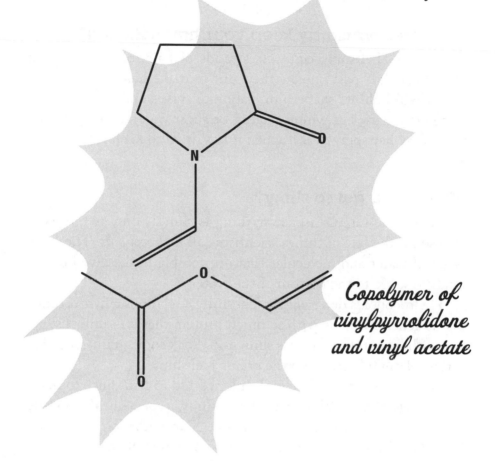

Copolymer of vinylpyrrolidone and vinyl acetate

used to keep the can from rusting inside, such as aminomethyl propanol or cyclohexylamine.

Hairsprays may also include emollients (skin softeners) such as cyclopentasyloxane. Dimethyl stearamine is sometimes added to reduce static electricity (by making the hair surface conduct electricity better). Many fragrant chemicals may also be added, such as linalool, limonene, butylphenyl methylpropional, amyl cinnamal, hexyl cinnamal, citronellol, or geraniol. These are citrus and floral scent molecules. Some hairsprays contain sunscreens such as ethylhexyl methoxycinnamate.

How does hairspray keep your hair stiffened?

The glue in hairspray connects strands of hair together, so that they don't slide past one another. But to make hair really stiff so that it will hold its shape into elaborate spikes and other shapes, some people use egg white, gelatin, or sugar water as the glue and then spray hairspray over it when it has dried to keep it from feeling sticky.

Why is hair gel so slimy?

For much the same reasons anything is slimy. Slimy is the word we use for the feel of things scientists call *hydrocolloids*. These are made of water and molecules that are too big to dissolve but too small to settle to the bottom of the water.

Hydrocolloids don't *always* feel slimy. Gelatin is a hydrocolloid that is generally made with so much protein that it is almost solid. But with less protein, it feels slimy too. Soak some grains of unflavored gelatin in water, and the grains feel slimy.

Pectin—the starch-like molecule we add to fruit juice to make jelly—feels slimy. White glue feels slimy, especially if you add borax to make slime. (See the project "Fun with Boron" on page 192.) The slime that snails make is also a hydrocolloid.

If you remove some water from a hydrocolloid, it usually gels. That is, it becomes more solid. This characteristic is useful in a hair product, since it helps the product stay in the hair and not run down the back of your neck. It is solid enough to hold in your hand without dripping but becomes more liquid as you rub it into your hair.

How a hydrocolloid reacts to the stress of working it into your hair depends on the nature of the particles in the water. Corn starch hydrocolloids are famous for becoming thick and almost solid when you hit them suddenly, while being almost completely liquid if you move your finger through them slowly. Hair gel is designed with smaller particles that have the opposite behavior. Hair gel thins when stressed, so it can be worked into the hair.

How does hair gel work?

Like hairspray, hair gel is made of polymers. The polymers are water soluble and tend to have positively charged areas that are attracted to the negatively charged areas of the hair strand.

As the gel is applied, the long strands of the polymers wrap around the hair strands and bind them together. When the gel dries, the polymers shrink around the strands of hair, pulling them tightly together.

Hair gels usually contain alcohol so they dry faster. Other ingredients include plasticizers (like the ones in hairspray) that keep the polymers soft and elastic, and usually some type of fragrance. Sunscreens are another common additive.

The main gelling agent is often a vegetable gum, such as guar gum. Other vegetable gums, such as marshmallow and aloe vera, are sometimes used. For extra hold and support for elaborate hairstyles, acrylic plastic polymers (similar to floor polish and white glue) are used. Humectants (molecules that absorb water from the air) are used to keep the gel from completely drying out and feeling crusty. The simplest ones are just sugars, such as agave nectar.

How does Biosilk keep your hair smooth?

Silicones. Although that particular brand name includes shampoos and hairsprays, only conditioners and detanglers are talked about in this section. To allow wet hair strands to easily slide past one another, conditioners and detanglers use two strategies.

First, they have ingredients that make the tiny scales on the hair shaft lie down, so they don't have rough surfaces that grip other hair shafts. Citric acid is sometimes used for this purpose.

Second, they coat the hair shaft with slippery oils and silicones to make the hair shafts glide across one another easily during combing and brushing.

In Biosilk, cyclomethicone and dimethicone are the slippery silicone oils that help the strands untangle.

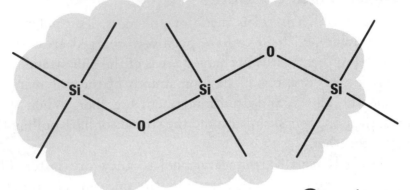

Dimethicone

These are often used in other products as carrier fluids in hairsprays or as skin protectants to act as a moisture barrier and prevent chafing.

Conditioners that you leave in the hair (instead of rinsing out) will contain mostly silicones and alcohol. To make the silicones feel less greasy, alkyl benzoates such as lauryl benzoate are used.

Alkyl benzoates are lubricants themselves and also serve as solvents to carry sunscreens, and they are emollients, keeping the skin from drying out. Alkyl

Lauryl benzoate

benzoates are esters, compounds that result when an alcohol reacts with an acid, in this case a fatty acid from vegetable oil. The alcohol end (the hexagonal benzyl alcohol at the bottom of the drawing) modifies the fatty end, so that it can join together oils and silicones and also help retain the fragrance molecules.

Why are there so many chemicals in makeup?

Because we want the makeup to do so many things.

Many of the ingredients are dyes and pigments to change the color of the skin or hair. Then something is needed to make the colors easy to apply to the skin, so carriers and propellants are added. Sunscreens are also needed to protect the skin from the sun, emollients and humectants to keep the skin from drying out, and preservatives to give the makeup longer shelf life.

Chemists could use oils in the makeup, but those can cause acne, so they modify the oils by making esters out of the fatty acids to get an oil-free makeup that does not cause the skin to break out. (See the lauryl benzoate molecule on the previous question for an example.)

Some makeups have both fat-soluble ingredients and water-soluble ingredients. To get these to mix and not separate like oil and vinegar dressing, *emulsifiers* are added to make something closer to a mayonnaise out of the watery and oily parts. An emulsifier is like a detergent—it is a molecule with one end that sticks to oil while the other end sticks to water.

A lot of the chemicals in makeup are perfumes.

Hexyl cinnamic aldehyde is the name for the scent in oil of chamomile, and it is one of the molecules that give chamomile tea its aroma and flavor. To keep the fragrances in the makeup and to keep them on the skin, fixatives are added. One fragrance fixative is an ester of benzyl alcohol and benzoic acid called benzyl benzoate.

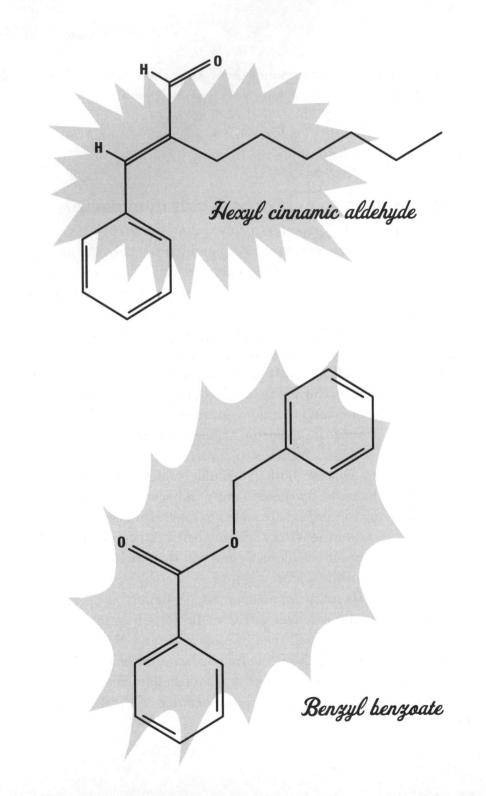

Hexyl cinnamic aldehyde

Benzyl benzoate

Benzyl benzoate also has the side effect of being an insecticide that kills skin mites that can cause the disease scabies.

What happens if chemicals get in your lungs?

The reason we breathe is to get oxygen into our lungs. But we also breathe to get chemicals such as carbon dioxide out of our bodies.

The lining of our nose and throat contain mucus and cilliary cells that trap and remove particles of dust in the air we breathe. These get several chances to remove particles, since the air moves past them as we breathe in and out, and the dust particles have a good chance of being collected before they actually touch the surface of the lung.

When smokers inhale cigarette smoke, it is to get the chemical nicotine into their lungs, where it then enters the bloodstream and is carried to the brain. Other molecules from smoke also enter the blood this way, such as carbon monoxide. It holds on to the hemoglobin (the protein that carries oxygen) in the blood more strongly than oxygen does, so less oxygen gets to the brain and muscles.

Other molecules in smoke get into the bloodstream or lodge in the lungs, where they can cause lung cancer or cancer of the mouth, throat, and larynx.

Some chemicals around the house are very irritating to breathe. Ammonia and bleach both contain strong alkalis that can damage the cells they contact. Some metal polishes contain acids that also damage cells.

Some chemicals can make you dizzy or cause unconsciousness. Doctors and dentists have you breathe molecules like nitrous oxide (laughing gas) or halothane to make you sleep through what would otherwise be a painfully unpleasant experience.

What is shoe polish made of?

Shoe polish is made from waxes, oils, naphtha, turpentine, ethylene glycol, and vegetable gums. It was originally invented as a waterproofing material for leather shoes. Later, people discovered that shoes could be given an attractive, glossy appearance with polish and buffing, and shiny shoes became fashionable.

Waxes like carnauba wax and beeswax help repel water and add shine. But to help them attach to leather, emulsifiers such as lanolin and ethylene glycol are added. These also allow the waxes, oils, and solvents to mix with water to form a thick butter-like emulsion that makes the waxy paste easier to apply to shoes. To thicken the emulsion, vegetable gums such as gum arabic are added.

Naphtha is a petroleum-based solvent that dissolves the wax to make it easier to apply. Turpentine is a similar solvent distilled from the sap of pine trees. Both of these dry quickly, allowing the waxes to harden on the surface of the leather while retaining their shiny, hard surfaces.

Shoe polish is colored by adding a form of fine carbon particles called lampblack for black polish and other dyes or pigments for other colors.

How does face paint stay moist?

Mineral oil. When people talk about oil paints "drying," they aren't actually talking about the same process by which a wet towel dries.

When oil paints react with oxygen in the air, they *polymerize*. That means the molecules link up into very long chains, becoming a solid but flexible plastic film. The pigment particles in the film of oil become trapped in the plastic film, which sticks to the surface it is painted on.

You would not want paint on a barn or on a canvas to stay oily and wet. But face paints are different—they are designed not to harden into a plastic. To do this, they are made from oils that don't oxidize in air. These oils are made from petroleum and are called mineral oils.

Face paints are mostly talcum powder mixed with mineral oil and pigments. To get them to stick to the skin, some lanolin, cetyl alcohol, triethanolamine, and some fatty acids are added, all of which have molecules where one end is attracted to oil and the other end is attracted to water and the proteins in the skin.

These ingredients help the face paint wash off (several of them are detergents and emulsifiers), and some react with air at the surface of the paint just like regular oil paint, to make a drier surface that does not transfer easily if touched.

How does Shout work?

Pre-soak stain removers are used when clothing has a stain that we expect will be too difficult for normal laundry detergent to remove.

Normal laundry detergents often contain inexpensive *ionic surfactants* (such as sodium laureth sulfate) that work best in warm or hot water. But hot water can help set some stains. A spray-on presoak stain remover like Shout has nonionic surfactants that start to work cold, as soon as they are sprayed on. *Nonionic surfactants* work in hard water (unlike many ionic surfactants), work in acid or alkaline solutions, and have good cleaning, foaming, and emulsifying properties that can be delicately tuned by controlling how the molecule is made.

Tuning these surfactants is a matter of controlling how long the water-loving end is and how long the oil-loving end is.

In the drawings shown on this page and the next, three different *polyethoxylated linear alcohols* are shown. These are

Laureth-3

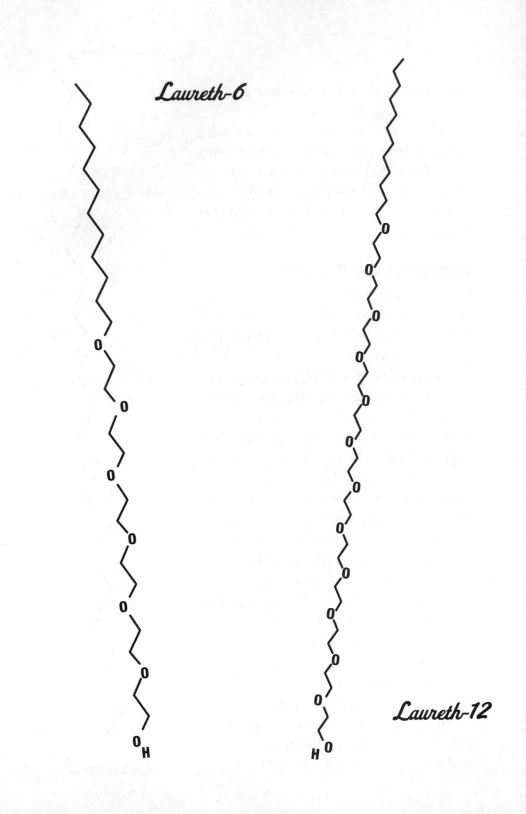

Laureth-6

Laureth-12

nonionic surfactants that are designed to have different lengths of water-loving ends (the ends on the bottom). Lauryl alcohol is the base. It is the chain of 12 carbon atoms on the top of the molecule. It dissolves in fats and oils.

The bottom of the molecule has (in these three cases) 3, 6, or 12 molecules of ethylene oxide added. The more ethylene oxide a molecule has, the more easily it will dissolve in water.

Molecules with less than 10 ethylene oxide units dissolve mainly in fats and oils. Those with more than 10 are water soluble. Those with 7 to 11 ethylene oxides are good for making water-in-oil emulsions (similar to butter or margarine). Those with 12 to 16 units are good for making oil-in-water emulsions (like mayonnaise). Those with 11 to 14 units are good for allowing water to wet fabrics easily. Those with 12 to 15 units make good detergents.

Shout uses several polyethoxylated linear alcohols for their different properties. Some smaller ones are used to lift oils from the fabric. Some larger ones are used to keep the oils in the water after they have been lifted off.

The alcohols can be linear (all in a line, as in the lauryl alcohol shown) or branched or have more complicated structure that includes cyclic molecules (loops). Linear alcohols are used where we want the detergent to break down easily in the environment. They pollute less, because bacteria can eat them easily.

Some formulas of Shout also include enzymes that help break down the proteins in blood and grass stains, and acrylic polymers to help them stay on the stain longer while in the washing machine.

4

Health and Safety

Humans use a lot of chemistry to keep healthy and safe. They have disinfectants for kitchen and bathroom surfaces but also for their skin. They protect it with lotions and creams and wash off germs (and the things germs eat) to stay healthy.

People also protect themselves from the chemicals they use. After all, we are made of chemicals, and chemicals react with one another. Knowing something about how chemicals behave can keep us safe while we use them.

Why do people need to wear goggles while they are doing experiments?

Because they want to keep their eyesight. Many experiments in chemistry are fairly safe. When we do experiments with food, for example, we usually don't need to wear protective eyewear. If a little salt or pepper gets in your eye, it might hurt, but the tears that come will safely wash the food away. But when we start to do experiments with chemicals such as acids, alkalis, or abrasive powders or when we heat something up, we want to protect our eyes from the hot or caustic materials.

We also wear protective gloves when we work with some chemicals or when we work with hot things. But while the skin on your hands might heal and only leave a scar, that doesn't stop you from using your hands. Damage to the eyes does not heal as easily, and you can have permanent damage to your vision.

Protective clothing is a good idea when working with most chemicals. It doesn't hurt to be safer than you need to be, and some experiments with harmless chemicals might produce things that are harmful. Keeping long hair away from flames is a good idea—tie your hair back so it doesn't fall into the flame.

Most protection is common sense. We wear gloves when using strong household cleansers like bleach. We wear dust masks when using sandpaper on plaster walls or when spraying paint. We wear eye protection whenever there is a danger of flying particles or droplets getting into our eyes.

Why does Bactine sting when you spray it on a cut?

Actually, Bactine is designed not to sting. It has lidocaine in it, similar to the novocaine the dentist uses to numb teeth. The germ-killing ingredient is benzalkonium chloride.

This disinfectant is used in many other products, such as Lysol, antiseptic towelettes, and newer non-alcohol-based hand sanitizers. It works by disrupting the cell walls of bacteria and disabling their enzymes, due to its action as a surfactant.

As a replacement for alcohol and hydrogen peroxide, benzalkonium chloride is used because it irritates the wound less. It is even used as a preservative in some eye drops and nasal sprays. Alcohol kills germs by drying them out, and other disinfectants (hydrogen peroxide, iodine, chlorhexidine) act by oxidizing (burning) germs. Both of those actions also harm skin cells and can cause stinging.

Lidocaine is used as the local anesthetic in Bactine because it acts very quickly. When the disinfectant is first sprayed on the cut

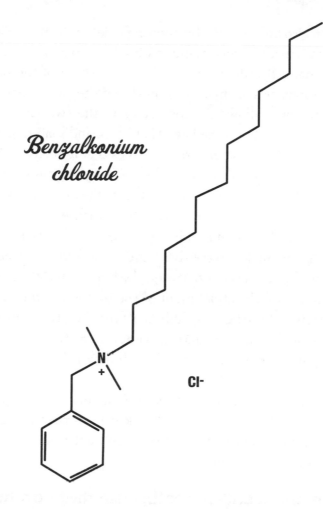

Benzalkonium chloride

or scrape, the temperature difference and the initial contact can stimulate pain nerves. But the lidocaine should quickly quiet them down.

How does soap get germs off you?

Your skin has a natural protective layer of oil that keeps it from drying out and keeps it flexible. If there are bacteria on top of this layer of natural oil, washing with soap will remove both the oil and the bacteria that sits on top.

Soap can also kill bacteria, by opening holes in the bacterial membrane, which is made of surfactants itself, like soap is. The surfactants in the bacterial cell wall are in two layers, with all of the oil-loving ends of the molecules facing inward between the two layers. Adding soap and scrubbing allows the molecules in the two layers to turn inside-out, and this allows the bacteria to leak and soap to get inside, where it can harm the bacterium's enzymes that it needs to live.

Many bacteria stick to surfaces by creating what is called a *biofilm*. This is a film of polymers that act as a glue or slime to hold the bacteria together and help them stick to a surface.

Soap can interfere with biofilms in several ways. It can attach to the molecules that make up the slime and allow it to be washed away, it can disrupt the attachment between the biofilm and the surface, or it can interfere with the attachment of the bacteria to the film.

Once bacteria have been scrubbed off the skin, the soap attaches to the walls of the bacteria and prevents them from attaching to the skin or one another. They then wash down the drain with the rinse water.

Some hand soaps also contain antibacterial chemicals such as triclosan or hexachlorophene that kill bacteria through other mechanisms. The combination of soap and antibacterial agents is better than either one alone.

Are there chemicals in toothpaste that can hurt you?

and . . .

Why can't you swallow toothpaste when you can swallow a mint?

It is not recommended that you swallow toothpaste. This is why children under six are not supposed to use regular toothpaste.

The main bioactive ingredient in toothpaste is sodium or tin fluoride. A tube of toothpaste contains enough fluoride to kill a six-year-old, and since toothpastes can come in flavors like bubble gum or watermelon, they should be kept away from young children. That said, few problems are actually reported, and the problems have not been fatal, even when severe.

Fluorides can damage the lining of the stomach and usually cause vomiting, whereby most of the toothpaste is eliminated and not absorbed into the bloodstream.

Toothpaste made for young children does not contain fluoride and is safe to swallow. Since their teeth are temporary anyway, the lack of fluoride is not a long-term health problem.

Why do your eyes hurt when you get out of the pool because you weren't wearing goggles?

If the pool water is properly maintained, they shouldn't. People add chemicals to swimming pool water to control microbes such as bacteria and algae. Chlorine can irritate eyes, but when that happens it's usually an indication that too much was used. A chemical called cyanuric acid is added to pool water to protect pool chlorine from sunlight. Cyanuric acid forms a weak bond with free chlorine in the pool water, preventing it from evaporating out of the pool. It also keeps free chlorine from irritating your eyes.

If there is too little chlorine in the pool water, this can cause cloudiness and the production of chloramines (that is what smells like chlorine to your nose). These can cause eye irritation.

Other things that can irritate the eyes are pH imbalances and hard water. We add acid or alkali to swimming pool water to adjust the pH to a neutral level. If this is done properly and often enough, eye irritation due to acidic or alkaline water will not be a problem.

How do face wipes take away zits?

There are a number of mechanisms. First, just wiping off excess oil using a clean paper towel can help prevent acne. So the face wipes can help even if they have no other ingredients at all. Face wipes also include detergents that make the oils wash away easily. Some use alcohol to both remove oil and kill germs.

But the three main acne-fighting ingredients are salicylic acid, benzoyl peroxide, and benzalkonium chloride.

Benzalkonium chloride was discussed with Bactine earlier (page 80). It kills germs by breaking up their cell walls and disabling their enzymes.

Salicylic acid works by getting inside the hair follicles (the clumps of cells in the pore that create hair) and removing dead cells that can clog the pores. It causes the dead cells to swell up with water, helping push them out. It is thus useful for preventing acne in the first place and less useful for treating pimples that are already inflamed.

Benzoyl peroxide kills the primary type of acne-forming bacteria, *Propionibacterium acnes*. It is thus the opposite of salicylic acid, in that it is good for inflamed pimples and doesn't do much for blackheads and whiteheads. Benzoyl peroxide kills germs by breaking down and releasing free oxygen, which burns the bacterial proteins. Bacteria cannot develop resistance to this type of antibacterial agent.

Benzoyl peroxide may also act as an irritant, causing the cells in the pores to grow faster and slough off faster, pushing out the waxy sebum that plugs up the pore. Because benzoyl peroxide dissolves in fats, it can penetrate into the sebum and get into the pore, where water-based medicines cannot.

How can Zanfel soap get off poison oak?

Zanfel is a cream that contains several strong surfactants (detergents) and tiny polyethylene beads. The main detergent in Zanfel is sodium lauroyl sarcosinate.

This detergent has a capability we have not discussed in other detergents. It is a *penetration enhancer*. That means it helps other molecules penetrate deeper into the skin. It is an ionic surfactant (you can see the plus sign by the sodium ion and the minus sign by the oxygen). It is derived from coconut oil and cleans without completely stripping the skin of all oils.

The second detergent in Zanfel is nonoxynol-9.

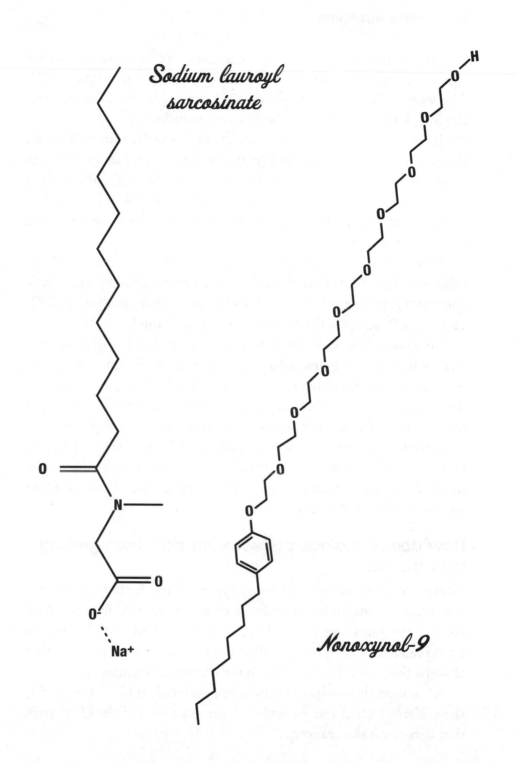

Sodium lauroyl sarcosinate

Nonoxynol-9

Nonoxynol-9 is a nonionic detergent. We saw these earlier when we discussed laureth-12 in Shout stain remover (page 75). The long chain of nine ethylene oxide groups is water-loving, and the long fatty acid chain at the bottom is oil-loving.

In the section on another surfactant, benzalkonium chloride, the antiseptic in Bactine (page 80), the discussion mentioned that some surfactants are good at breaking up cell walls and killing microbes. The same thing happens with nonoxynol-9: it is used in Zanfel to break up the poison *urushiol* that causes poison ivy and poison oak rashes.

Nonoxynol-9 is a polyethylene glycol. The long chain with all ethylene oxide units (two carbons and an oxygen) is the polyethylene part (*poly* means "many"). Another polyethylene glycol is C12-15 Pareth-9, and it is the third detergent in Zanfel.

To make these detergents work better in hard water, sodium EDTA is added. It grabs onto magnesium and calcium ions in the water and keeps them from interfering with the detergents. To keep the detergents from spoiling, a *bactericide* (bacteria killer) called quaternium-15 is used. It releases formaldehyde to kill germs.

Another surfactant, triethanolamine (which is three ethylene molecules all attached to a central nitrogen atom) helps make the urushiol soluble in water. It also adjusts the acidity of the product and neutralizes fatty acids.

How does sunblock protect your skin from getting sunburned?

There are actually two different types of products that protect against sunburn: sunblock and sunscreen. *Sunscreen* absorbs ultraviolet light and turns it into heat. Molecules that absorb particular wavelengths of light are called dyes. A sunscreen is a dye that absorbs the invisible ultraviolet light that causes sunburn.

One such dye molecule is benzophenone-3. It blocks primarily the UVB light that causes sunburn but not much of the UVA light that can cause skin cancer.

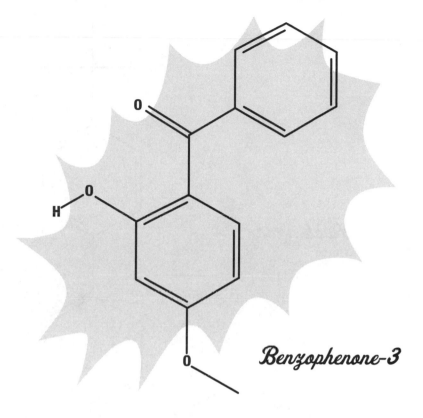

Benzophenone-3

Another sunscreen, avobenzone, is better at blocking both forms of ultraviolet light. There are at least 23 other similar compounds that act in much the same way.

A different type of protection is offered by *sunblock*. In a sunblock, the ultraviolet light is reflected instead of being absorbed. In some sunblocks, almost all light is reflected, including visible light, so the product looks bright white. In others, the size of the reflecting particles in the cream is carefully selected so that visible light is not reflected and the skin colors are not blocked.

Sunblocks typically include the same pigments used in white paint, specifically titanium dioxide and zinc oxide. Zinc oxide is

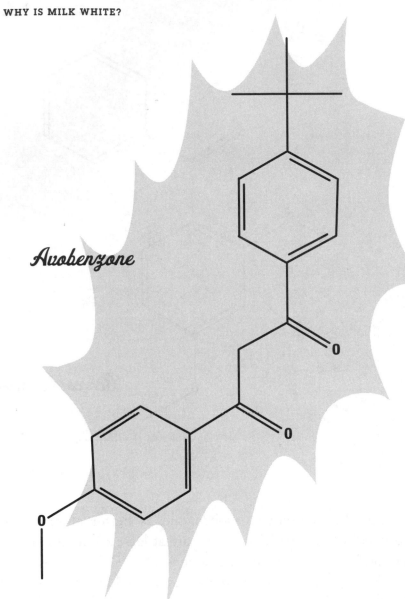

Avobenzone

better at blocking the entire ultraviolet spectrum than titanium dioxide.

How do you get sunburned when it is cloudy?

You may have noticed that on a cloudy day you can still see things. The sky is not totally dark, like it is at night. This shows us that some light is getting through the clouds. That light includes ultraviolet light that can cause sunburn and skin cancer.

Cloudy days are usually cooler, so the skin does not feel warm and there is less of an urge to get into the shade or go indoors to cool off. So you might actually stay outdoors for a longer period. If you are at the beach on a cloudy day, you may be wearing less clothing, allowing more light to get to your skin.

Also, on cloudy days, you may not remember to use sunscreen.

How do you get a tan?

You get a tan by damaging your skin. People need sunlight to produce vitamin D. As humans moved from Africa into northern countries that did not get enough sunlight to produce adequate vitamin D, they evolved to produce less of the protective melanin pigment that blocks ultraviolet radiation and the damage it can cause.

Instead of producing melanin pigment in their skin all the time, light-skinned people only produce a little, unless the skin detects damage from ultraviolet light. Then it starts producing more melanin. It takes about three days for the melanin to be produced, so if there is a lot of sun exposure before the tan is produced, you will get sunburned.

When you tan, you get a little bit of tanning effect right away, because the longer wavelength UVA light causes damage to what melanin exists, causing it to combine with oxygen. This makes it darker. But most of the tan comes from increased production of melanin, which takes longer.

The color of your skin without melanin can be seen inside your mouth. The pink color is due to the color of the blood flowing in the fine capillaries (tiny blood vessels) and the scattering of light by the skin cells, which would look white if it were not for the red blood. The red and the white combine to look pink.

Ultraviolet light damages skin in several ways. It breaks up DNA, which is why it can cause cancer. It is the products of DNA destruction that trigger the tanning process, so you can't get a tan without first damaging your skin and risking cancer. But the sun also damages the proteins that make skin flexible. This results in dry and wrinkled skin, an effect called *premature aging*, since it makes people who are in the sun a lot look much older than people who get less sun.

Since we can now get vitamin D from milk and supplements and we have effective sunscreens (and clothing and hats), there is little reason to risk cancer by excessive sun exposure.

Why does hydrogen peroxide bubble up when you put it on your cut?

and . . .

Why is it when you put hydrogen peroxide in your mouth it bubbles?

Hydrogen peroxide is H_2O_2. You can see that this is water (H_2O) with an extra oxygen atom attached. Catalysts in your blood called *peroxidases* and *catalases* break it into water and oxygen.

Catalase is an enzyme (a protein the body makes that speeds up chemical reactions). It is very effective at speeding up the natural breakdown of hydrogen peroxide into oxygen and water. In each second, a molecule of catalase can break down 40 million molecules of hydrogen peroxide.

Your cells produce hydrogen peroxide as an undesirable side effect of breathing oxygen. Hydrogen peroxide is dangerous to cells, so they produce catalase to quickly break it down and escape damage. When you have damaged your skin, the cells that produce catalase are exposed. When you add hydrogen peroxide, the catalase in the cells breaks it down, and bubbles of oxygen form.

Hydrogen peroxide is used to damage germs that might find their way into damaged skin. If you use lots of hydrogen peroxide, the catalase can't keep up, and the bacteria get damaged. Some skin cells also get damaged, which is why the peroxide stings a little, and peroxide is no longer recommended as a disinfectant for wounds now that better alternatives are available.

Other organisms also breathe oxygen, and so they need their own catalase enzymes. You can see them in action if you add some dried yeast to a cup of hydrogen peroxide. The peroxide starts to bubble vigorously as the oxygen is produced.

Why does cough syrup have a strong taste, and how does it make you stop coughing?

The active ingredients in cough syrup are drugs derived from opium. Coughing is caused by the brain, and these drugs act on the brain to suppress the urge to cough.

Opiates are a type of bitter-tasting chemicals called alkaloids. These are molecules that contain basic (alkaline) nitrogen atoms. Some alkaloids you may know include caffeine, nicotine, codeine, and quinine. Others are cocaine, morphine, heroin, ephedrine, atropine, dextromethorphan, pseudoephedrine, and strychnine.

Because the ingredients are bitter tasting, cough syrups have strong flavors to mask the bitterness. But that is not the only reason cough syrups are unpleasant to use. Because the ingredients in cough syrup include things like dextromethorphan and codeine, which are used by some people as recreational drugs, the pill forms have been taken off the market. Instead, the syrup forms are available, since they are much harder to use for purposes other than preventing coughs.

In other words, cough syrups taste bad on purpose, so people don't misuse them.

Why are some medicines liquid and some medicines pills?

Besides preventing people from misusing certain drugs, liquid drug delivery systems are sometimes preferred because they are faster acting than pills. An extreme example is nasal spray, which acts very quickly because it can be delivered right into the nose and then to the brain, without first having to be digested in the stomach and intestines to get into the bloodstream.

Pills make bad tasting medicines easy to swallow, since only a little of the medicine actually touches the tongue before the pill is swallowed. But pills and capsules can also be designed to pass through the acidic stomach without being harmed, so they can dissolve in the alkaline intestines and be absorbed into the bloodstream. Stomach acids can break down some medicines and prevent them from doing their job.

Pills and capsules can also be designed to dissolve slowly, so that they release small amounts of the medicine over a long period of time. This allows the patient to take one pill and get relief from symptoms for a whole day.

Some things we take in pill form are liquids. An example is vitamin A. It can be absorbed into powder to make a pill, but it can also be enclosed in a soft gelatin capsule that dissolves in the stomach to release the oily liquid vitamin.

How do Band-Aids stick to your skin?

There are several things going on that make the Band-Aid stick. This is true of almost any glue.

Mechanical adhesion is like Velcro. Two rough surfaces have many little places that catch onto one another, like hooks catch loops.

Electrical adhesion is where one part of a molecule is positively charged and is attracted to the negative charges of another molecule. It is a form of chemical adhesion, in which chemical bonds are formed between the glue and the surfaces that are being glued.

Atmospheric adhesion is like suction cups. Air pressure holds suction cups to smooth surfaces like glass.

To be a good glue, something must stick well to the surface it is applied to (this is called *adhesion*). But it must also stick well to itself (this is called *cohesion*). For example, water has good adhesion. You can wet two pieces of paper and glue them together with just water. But water does not have good cohesion, and you can pull the pieces of paper apart and water will remain on both of them, because the water did not stick well to itself.

In a Band-Aid, you want the glue to stick very well to the Band-Aid and pretty well to itself, but you don't want it sticking too well to the skin or it will hurt to pull it off, and there might be some glue left on the skin that you would have to wash off later.

So Band-Aids have a special glue that doesn't hold on to the skin as well as superglue would. But it holds on to the skin a little better than sticky tape used for paper would, so the Band-Aid stays on long enough to do its job.

What are some chemicals that make people crazy?

Psychologists use the term *psychosis* instead of "crazy." The brain works by using chemicals to send signals between nerve cells. As mentioned in chapter 1, these chemicals are called *neurotransmitters*. If a person has a lack of some neurotransmitters or an excess of one or more neurotransmitters, they may perceive things differently from other people.

One example of this is hallucinations, where they see or hear things that are not there. But other examples are more common, such as depression and bipolar disorders, where the person feels sad or irritable or has an elevated arousal or energy level.

Some drugs affect the same receptors in the brain that natural neurotransmitters affect. This is why they have effects on the brain and why we use them to make up for a lack of a neurotransmitter in people whose bodies aren't making enough. Other drugs block the receptors that neurotransmitters use, so the person experiences the same effects as if they had little or none of the neurotransmitter.

Drugs that can strongly affect how the brain reacts to neurotransmitters are called *psychotomimetic drugs*. This just means that they mimic the effects of psychosis. Often these drugs are used (or abused) in small doses that do not trigger psychotic effects or behavior, but if taken in large doses the effects can be disabling.

An example is tetrahydrocannabinol, the active ingredient in marijuana. In massive doses taken intravenously, it affects the cannabinoid receptors in the brain to such an extent that symptoms of schizophrenia develop. Some opiates are also psychotomimetic, such as pentazocine and butophanol. Other alkaloids that can be psychotomimetic are scopolamine, atropine, diphenhydramine, phencyclidine, and dextromethorphan. Psychotomimetic drugs may cause symptoms of depression or euphoria and dreamlike states in which things are not clear and sharp.

What happens if you breathe in hairspray?

Most of the contents of hairspray are propellants and carrier fluids. Some propellants and carriers, such as hydrofluorocarbons and silicones, are fairly harmless and merely reduce the amount of oxygen you breathe. This can make you dizzy, like holding your breath. These are called *asphyxiants*.

Some common propellants like nitrous oxide, propane, and butane can actually affect how the brain works. Carrier fluids like alcohol and ether also affect the brain. The effects are caused by either stimulating or blocking receptors in the brain that are normally triggered by natural neurotransmitters.

The effects can be drowsiness or sleep, distortion of vision or hearing, emotional disturbances, or hallucinations. Other, more common effects are headache, nausea and vomiting, slurred speech, loss of control of the muscles and coordination, and wheezing. Prolonged or frequent breathing of aerosol propellants and carriers can result in rashes around the skin areas that are exposed to the chemical.

Death from asphyxiation (lack of oxygen) or from heart failure can result if large amounts of aerosol propellants are inhaled. But since aerosol propellants also get very cold as they expand, they can freeze the delicate tissues in the lungs, nose, and throat. The lack of motor control can cause the person to inhale vomit and choke on it. Brain damage can also occur with prolonged inhalation. But breathing a little bit while using the hairspray is generally not a problem.

Why do people use hydrogen peroxide for mouth rinse?

Hydrogen peroxide kills the germs that cause gum disease and helps remove particles of food and bacteria from between teeth. It also reacts with bad-smelling molecules that are produced by bacteria, so it freshens breath.

Brushing your teeth is good for removing the bacteria that have glued themselves to your tooth surfaces. It also reaches down into the space between the tooth and the gum to remove some of the food and bacteria that settle there. But it is not very good at getting deep below the gum line.

Flossing helps a lot. It scrapes off the biofilm that the bacteria use to glue themselves to the teeth, and the floss can slip way down between the teeth and the gums to reach where the toothbrush can't. Still, flossing can leave many of the germs behind.

Hydrogen peroxide reacts with the catalase enzymes that the germs produce, causing it to split into water and oxygen. The bubbles of oxygen then carry the bacteria and food particles up out of the gums where they can be spit out. There is so much hydrogen peroxide in a mouthful that it overwhelms the bacteria's ability to break it down, and the bacteria are killed.

Because the peroxide works by oxidizing the bacterial cell walls and contents, there is little that bacteria can do to develop resistance to it. This is unlike many other antibiotics, which work by targeting specific functions in the germs. The germs can evolve defenses against these more easily than they can against hydrogen peroxide.

What happens when you swallow hydrogen peroxide?

That's not a good thing to do. Though the body produces hydrogen peroxide as a byproduct of cellular metabolism (breathing) and has catalase enzymes to break it down, swallowing a mouthful of peroxide will overwhelm the ability of the catalase to work. This will allow the remaining peroxide to damage cells in the same way it damages bacteria. The result is a sore throat and an upset stomach.

The peroxide will also continue to break down as the body produces more catalase enzyme, so you will get bubbles of oxygen gas forming in your stomach, which will cause you to burp.

How does hydrogen peroxide bleach your hair?

Hydrogen peroxide oxidizes the eumelanin and pheomelanin pigments in hair. By itself, hydrogen peroxide will do some lightening, but for hair bleaching it is usually combined with ammonia. While any alkali will make the scales on the hair shaft open up to let the peroxide in, ammonia actually breaks down the little packages (called *melanosomes*) of melanin particles, allowing the bleach better access to them.

Melanins come in many forms, but most are similar to the molecule shown in the drawing on the next page. Like any dye or pigment, the ability to absorb a particular color comes from the alternating single and double bonds. Single bonds are shown in the picture as single lines, and double bonds are double lines.

When a molecule has single and double bonds right next to one another, the electrons that form the bonds usually spread out over both locations, so we actually think of the two bonds as being "one and a half" bonds. This is important, because in a dye these "delocalized" electrons resonate with the light, at a frequency that depends on how many bonds they can cover.

If there are lots of delocalized electrons in a molecule, the light they absorb will have a long wavelength, like red or infrared. If

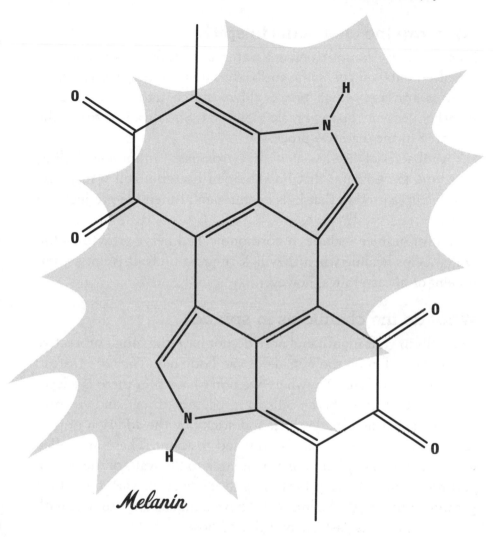

Melanin

there are only a few, the wavelength will be shorter, like blue or ultraviolet.

Reacting the molecule with hydrogen peroxide causes oxygen atoms to attach to the molecule. This usually turns one or more of the double bonds into single bonds. This means the molecule no longer absorbs light the same way and is either a different color or loses its color altogether.

What are the chemicals in spit?

Mostly water. About 98 percent water, in fact. Saliva also contains dissolved salts, mucus, some antibacterial molecules, and enzymes such as amylase, which breaks down starch into simple sugars. Another enzyme, lipase, breaks down fat. So saliva is actually the first step in the digestive process.

Antibacterial agents such as peroxidase, immunoglobulins, lysozyme (an enzyme that breaks open bacterial cell walls), and lactoferrin (a protein that kills bacteria and fungi) are produced in saliva.

Saliva in mice includes a hormone called nerve growth factor, which helps healing when they lick their wounds. It is not a component of human saliva, however.

What do the chemicals in spit do?

The cells in your mouth and nose do not have the tough protective barrier that skin on the outside of the body has. They are instead protected by mucus. Anywhere we don't have skin there is a layer of mucus that protects the cells from bacteria, fungi, and viruses.

Mucus is water made thick and sticky by the addition of proteins that have simple sugars attached to them. These are called glycoproteins. They help the mucus stick to the walls of the mouth and nose, and they trap bacteria and particles so that they don't get into your lungs. The lungs also have a mucus layer to deal with anything that gets past the mouth and nose.

Mucus lubricates the food we eat, so it is easier to chew and swallow. When you see, smell, or even think about food, your salivary glands start to produce fluids in anticipation of the need to moisten and lubricate the food you are about to eat.

The cells that line your nose and throat contain cells that constantly move mucus toward the back of the throat, where it can be swallowed, along with any particles and bacteria it has trapped.

Besides trapping bacteria, mucus contains enzymes that break open bacterial walls. The enzyme lysozyme and the protein lactoferrin are part of what is called the *innate immune system*. This is the system that works against any bacteria that comes along. The *adaptive immune system* recognizes germs so we don't get the same disease again.

Lactoferrin has oxidized iron (rust) in it that makes it look red when purified (but the amount in saliva is so small it does not have a color). Lactoferrin binds to bacterial cell walls, and the oxidized iron produces peroxides that break down the walls and cause the bacteria to leak.

Lactoferrin attracts white blood cells to bacteria, so they get eaten up. Its main function elsewhere in the body is to ferry iron around to where it is needed. But it has many other functions. In saliva, it binds iron that bacteria need to live so it is not available to them, it binds to the cell walls, it intrudes inside the bacterium, it releases peroxides, and it interferes with the enzymes in the bacteria or fungus.

Lactoferrin binds to the same sites on cells that viruses do, so it blocks viruses from entering cells. It also binds directly to some viruses, and it can prevent viruses from growing inside cells, by attracting natural killer cells and macrophages to come along and kill the infected cell.

What common chemicals shouldn't be mixed together?

Chlorine bleach is the first one that comes to mind. If an acid like vinegar is added to it, it produces poisonous and irritating gases such as chlorine and hydrogen chloride (which makes hydrochloric acid when it contacts the water in your eyes, throat, and nose).

Mixing bleach with ammonia can produce poisonous chloramine vapors.

Most of the strong chemicals in your house should not be mixed, if only because it makes them less effective. Oftentimes when strong chemicals are mixed together, they generate a lot of heat and can boil, splattering caustic chemicals onto your skin or into your eyes. Lye and drain cleaners have to be very carefully handled for this reason. They can boil the water they are added to.

Pesticides should never be mixed with anything other than what the label recommends for diluting them. They are poisons to start with, and causing a chemical reaction can liberate poisonous vapors or gases that you might not even be able to smell, so you might not know you are poisoning yourself.

5

Things That Catch Fire or Go Bang

Most people delight in fire and explosions of all kinds—fireworks, cap guns, birthday candles, sparklers—and an action movie without explosions is hard to find. I like to use this fascination, this "teaching moment," to explain the science behind the pyrotechnics. Each time a question is answered, a new questions pops up, and the budding scientist gains new understanding of her world.

How do explosives work?

An explosion happens when something burns so fast that it makes a bang. We usually see things burn in the open, where wood, paper, or some other burnable material gets the oxygen it needs from the air, just like we do. But an explosive carries its own oxygen in the compound. It keeps the oxygen right next to the ingredients that burn, so the burning can happen very quickly.

Some explosives are very easy to set off. The explosives in cap guns can be set off by just hitting them with the tiny hammer in the gun. Gunpowder can be set off with a match. Nitroglycerin will explode if you drop it on the floor.

To make explosives safer to use, it helps if they are harder to set off, so they only explode when we want them to. To make nitroglycerin safer to use, Alfred Nobel figured out how to let it soak into powdered clay. The result is dynamite, which won't explode if you just drop it on the floor. Inside a stick of dynamite is a little firecracker. When you light the fuse of the firecracker and the firecracker blows up, it has enough force to make the nitroglycerin explode.

There are many types of explosives in use today, and most of them are designed to be hard to set off. You can hit TNT with a hammer and it won't explode. Like dynamite, it needs a small explosive that is easier to ignite. This *primer* or *blasting cap* is often protected in a metal casing and triggered by electricity. This allows the explosive to be set off from a distance, using long wires or a timer.

How do you make explosives?

To make an explosive, you need to mix something that will burn (called the *fuel*), such as charcoal or sulfur, with something that provides oxygen (called the *oxidizer*). The closer you can get the fuel to the oxidizer, the faster it will burn.

One of the first explosives to be invented was gunpowder. The fuel is charcoal and sulfur. The oxidizer is potassium nitrate, which is a chemical that has three oxygen atoms in it. When it gets hot, it releases the oxygen, so the charcoal and the sulfur can burn.

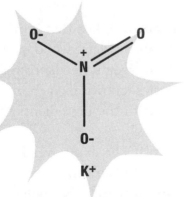

Potassium nitrate –
the oxidizer in gunpowder

To make sure the oxidizer and the fuel are very close to each other, each of them is ground into a fine powder, and then the powder is carefully mixed together. The finer you grind the powders, the better the gunpowder will be.

To keep the powders from separating, they are mixed with a

little water to make a paste and then dried out again, after which the dried paste is ground up. This makes the gunpowder more reliable and helps it all burn up at once.

Another way to make an explosion is to mix a fuel really well with air and then ignite it. Dust explosions happen when coal dust in a mine or flour dust in a mill are mixed into the air and then set off by a spark or a flame. Gas explosions happen in much the same way, when a flammable gas or vapor mixes very well with air and then gets ignited somehow.

Nitroglycerin and TNT are examples of what are called *high explosives*. In a high explosive, the fuel and oxidizer are packed into the same molecule. They are extremely close together. That makes nitroglycerin and TNT much more powerful than gunpowder.

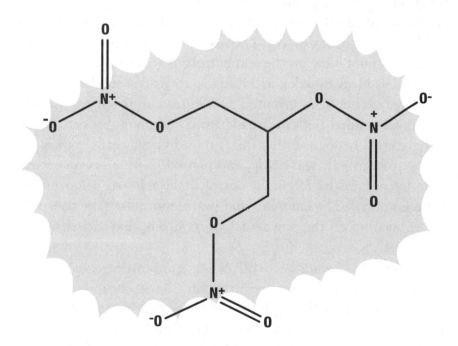

Nitroglycerine – the explosive in dynamite

When a high explosive detonates, the molecule comes apart and the atoms rearrange themselves. The oxygen combines with the fuel very quickly, and there is a big bang.

Not all explosives use oxygen as the oxidizer, however. Other elements can act like oxygen to burn fuels. Chlorine, fluorine, iodine, and bromine are all good oxidizers.

What types of chemicals are in gunpowder?

Gunpowder that is made from charcoal, sulfur, and potassium nitrate is called *black powder*. It is not used much anymore, because it makes a lot of smoke when it explodes. It also leaves a chemical residue in the gun barrel that makes it corrode.

To solve these problems, *smokeless powder* was invented. High explosives like guncotton (cellulose nitrate) were too powerful to use in guns and cannons. However, they could be diluted with alcohol or similar liquids to make a jelly that would harden and could be cut into tiny pieces. The result was a less powerful explosive that did not blow up the gun barrels. It was still three times as powerful as black powder, and it made very little smoke.

Alfred Nobel, who invented dynamite, also invented a smokeless powder called *Ballistite*, made from camphor, guncotton, and nitroglycerin. Later, a similar mixture of nitroglycerin, guncotton, and petroleum jelly was made, and named *Cordite* because it was made into grains by forcing it out of little holes so it looked like string (or cord). The camphor and petroleum jelly slow down the rate of burning, so the powder is not so strong that it destroys the gun barrel.

Modern *propellants* are still called gunpowder, even though they aren't powders. They are little balls, flakes, or rods, and they are often coated with graphite. Graphite is a gray powder form of carbon, and it conducts electricity. Conducting electricity is important, since it prevents static electricity from building up. A spark of static electricity could cause the gunpowder to ignite unexpectedly.

Is there chemistry in guns?

The chemistry used in guns is not limited to gunpowder. In order to make the gunpowder explode, a *primer* is needed. A primer is an explosive that will detonate when it is hit by the firing pin in the gun.

You may have seen "strike anywhere" matches, which burst into flame with just a little friction. They can also be lit by hitting them with a small hammer. They are made from sulfur and phosphorus, with an oxidizer that is more powerful than potassium nitrate, such as potassium chlorate. A mixture like that could be used as a primer in a bullet cartridge. But some specialized *contact explosives*—explosives that are easy to set off—have been invented for just this purpose.

One of the early contact explosives used in primers was mercury fulminate. It is not as corrosive as contact explosives made with potassium chlorate, so it did less damage to the gun.

Other contact explosives have replaced mercury fulminate as primers in modern weapons. Lead azide, lead styphnate, and a class of compounds called tetrazenes are now used. All of these contact explosives are molecules that come apart very easily and release a lot of energy very quickly when they come apart and the atoms rearrange themselves.

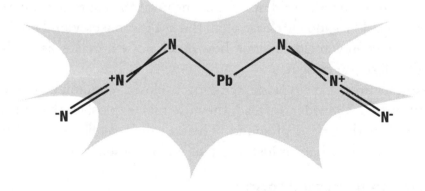

Lead azide – a contact explosive

What happens if you breathe in gunpowder?

You won't explode. Like any other dust, gunpowder is unpleasant to breathe in. You will cough and sneeze as your body tries to get rid of it.

The charcoal in black powder is not toxic. Sulfur is also fairly safe in the quantities you would inhale. Potassium nitrate is a lung irritant. None of the ingredients would be likely to be fatal if inhaled with a single breath, but it would not be fun. In general, I would recommend against inhaling powders of any sort.

Modern smokeless powders are not really powders and are much harder to inhale. Nitrocellulose might give you a headache. Nitroglycerin, on the other hand, affects the blood vessels, dilating them. This lowers blood pressure (which is why people with heart disease take nitroglycerin pills).

What makes a firework explode?

The first fireworks were made in China over a thousand years ago. They used the newly invented black powder as a propellant for rockets and as a noisemaker.

You need two things to make an exploding firecracker from black powder: the powder and a closed container. Black powder by itself will just burn—it won't explode. But if it is in a closed container, pressure will build up as it burns until the container bursts all at once. The sudden release of all the hot gas makes a loud noise. Just like when you close a door, how much noise it makes depends on how fast you close it.

Some fireworks explode without a closed container. These don't use black powder. Instead, they use high explosives that burn faster than the speed of sound. This is called *detonating*, and it breaks the sound barrier just like a jet making a sonic boom.

How are fireworks made?

Some simple fireworks, like sparklers, are safe enough to make at home. They are basically gunpowder recipes with added iron or aluminum to make the sparks and some sugar or starch in water to make a paste that sticks on the wire.

Firecrackers are gunpowder packed into cardboard tubes that act as the closed container needed to make noise. A fuse is often just gunpowder wrapped in tissue paper. The fuse burns slowly enough to let you get away from the firecracker before the gunpowder in the cardboard tube ignites and explodes.

Rockets are also often simple cardboard tubes filled with gunpowder, but with one end capped with a clay nozzle instead of being completely closed. When lit, the powder burns instead of exploding, and the hot gas comes out the nozzle. The force that it creates pushes the rocket away.

Mortars are small cannons made of cardboard tubes. A complex explosive device called a *shell* is lit and dropped into the tube. The bottom of the shell is a firecracker that explodes. This pushes the rest of the shell out of the tube into the air, where it can explode high above the spectators. It often has little bits of gunpowder called *stars*. These create the flower shapes as they burn brightly in the air after the shell explodes. The stars can have additives that make them burn brighter or burn in different colors.

Why are explosives so loud?

We hear sounds when air molecules push on our eardrums. The harder they push, the louder the sound.

To create sounds, air must be pushed. The faster the air is pushed, the more pressure that is created, since the air has less time to get out of the way.

If you push on the air with your hand, you can feel the pressure of the air on your face, but you won't hear any sound because your hand is moving too slowly. To make a sound, the air must move faster than it can get away. You can do this by clapping your hands together. That traps air between our hands, increasing the pressure. The air molecules can't get away fast enough, so they all get crowded together.

When an explosive is set off, it produces a lot of molecules of gas in a very short time. These molecules bounce into air molecules and make sound waves. The faster the explosive burns, the louder the sound waves will be.

A firecracker moves air faster than your clapping hands can move air, so it sounds louder than hand clapping. Dynamite explodes faster than gunpowder, so it makes an even louder sound.

How are explosives different from grenades?

Grenades are small devices that contain explosives and are launched or thrown so that they explode away from the person who threw them.

Hand grenades are thrown by hand. Other grenades have launchers. Some launchers attach to rifles, while others are carried by themselves, such as rocket propelled grenades, or RPGs.

Explosive grenades often have steel cases that are cut so that when the device explodes the bits of steel will act like bullets. These are called *fragmentation grenades*. Others called *concussion grenades* merely explode; they are meant to stun people.

Grenades use several chemical reactions to work. When the grenade leaves the thrower's hand, a spring pushes a pin down on a percussion cap. That cap explodes and lights a four-second fuse. That fuse eventually sets off a detonator, which then sets off the main explosive charge.

Not all grenades are actually explosive. Some are designed to set fires. These are called *incendiary grenades*. Others release smoke or tear gas or just make a loud noise or flash of light.

What do cap guns have in them that make them explode?

Several compounds can be used. A contact explosive made from phosphorus, sulfur, and potassium chlorate will explode when hit with the small hammer in a cap gun. This is similar to the mixture used in "strike anywhere" matches. An early formula (from 1926) used potassium chlorate, sulfur, and antimony. You can tell if a cap has sulfur in it by the smell it makes (like a struck match) when it explodes.

As mentioned on page 105, contact explosives are those that are easy to set off. They're made from compounds, such as potassium chlorate or potassium perchlorate, that are very good oxidizing agents. Fuels that are very easily oxidized, such as sulfur, phosphorus, or antimony, are added to the powerful oxidizer to create an explosive sensitive enough to be set off by the force of the hammer in the cap gun.

Other exploding toys, such as the "bang snaps" novelty fireworks, use a different contact explosive, a high explosive called silver fulminate. A tiny amount of silver fulminate is added to some sand, which is then wrapped in thin paper. When thrown at something, the explosive makes a loud bang, but the sand absorbs most of the energy, so no damage is done.

Fulminates are made by reacting gold, silver, mercury, or platinum with ammonia or nitric acid. Those metals don't react easily, and the compounds they create break apart easily, releasing energy. Most contact explosives use compounds that break apart easily and release energy. Other examples are ammonium triiodide, tri-acetone tri-peroxide, lead azide, and lead styphnate.

What makes flames turn colors?

One part of what makes hot things a certain color is just how hot they are. You can see this when you look at the wires in a toaster glowing from dull red to bright orange as they heat up. You can see the color of an incandescent light change as

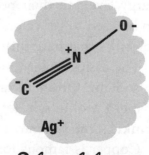

Silver fulminate
– *a contact explosive*

you move a dimmer switch from low to high. The dull orange of the lowest setting becomes the white hot of the highest setting.

In a flame from burning gas or alcohol, there are often two main colors, orange and blue, which are produced through different mechanisms. The orange comes from particles of unburned soot that glow from the heat. Their color is determined by the temperature in what is called *blackbody radiation*. Red is the coolest flame, then orange, yellow, white, and finally blue.

Blue color would indicate a temperature of over 10,000 degrees Celsius if the sooty part of the flame were that color. However, the blue part of the flame we normally see gets its color from a different mechanism. Electrons in atoms and molecules can be excited into higher energy levels as the gas or alcohol burns. These electrons can emit that energy as light when they fall back down to their normal energy levels. The color of light they emit indicates what molecules they are, since each molecule has a different energy level. The blue comes mainly from a molecule made from one carbon atom bonded to one hydrogen atom. Some of the light in the greenish-blue portion of the flame comes from a molecule made of two carbon atoms.

How do we make different colored fireworks?

As discussed in the answer to the previous question, the blue part of a gas flame comes from electrons falling from excited high energy levels to their normal lower levels. The same mechanism can be used to get colors other than blue—just add some atoms or molecules that have different energy levels.

The easiest color to add to a flame is bright yellow, from adding sodium. Ordinary table salt will work just fine. You can soak a paper towel in salt, let it dry, and then burn it. Or you can just sprinkle some salt into a gas flame.

Copper is famous for its blue- and green-colored compounds. If you put some copper compounds into a flame, you get pretty blues and greens. Lithium salts make red flames, and strontium salts make even brighter red flames. Barium salts make blue-green flames, and potassium makes violet flames. When you want to make fireworks with sparks of different colors, you can add these compounds to the burning materials.

Some burning materials make colors by other mechanisms. Magnesium burns with a bright white light, because it is hot enough to get into the white region of the blackbody radiation curve. Similarly, orange colors in fireworks are often made from glowing balls of carbon, hot enough to glow orange.

What is plasma?

Plasma is a gas that is so hot that the molecules or atoms lose some of their electrons. On Earth, the most common forms of matter are solid, liquid, and gas. But in the universe as a whole, the most common form of matter is plasma.

The sun is a big ball of plasma. Lightning is a plasma. The electric sparks you get from static electricity are made of plasma. There is a plasma inside every glowing fluorescent light tube and every neon light.

Plasmas consist of electrons and the positively charged atoms the electrons were stripped from. These atoms that are missing electrons are called ions, and we say that the gas that has become a plasma has been *ionized*. Gases that have only a small percentage of their atoms stripped of electrons are said to be weakly ionized. When more of the atoms are affected, the plasma is said to be highly ionized.

Most flames are weakly ionized plasmas. Sparks and lightning can be highly ionized.

Because electrons carry a negative charge and stripped atoms carry a positive charge, plasmas can conduct electricity. Gases do not conduct electricity.

Plasmas can emit colors just like flames do. The color of a neon light is due to excited electrons falling back into their normal energy levels, emitting light to lose the extra energy. Other plasmas emit other colors, since their atoms or molecules have different energy levels. Helium plasmas are pink. Plasmas made from sodium vapor are the characteristic yellow of sodium.

How do you make a volcano with chemicals?

Most of the volcanoes made for grade-school science fair projects are made using a baking soda and vinegar reaction to create a foam to represent the lava. Dishwashing soap is often added, along with food coloring, to get a red or orange appearance.

Baking soda is a salt made from a strong base and a weak acid. The strong base is sodium hydroxide, and the weak acid is carbon dioxide dissolved in water, the same thing you drink in soda water.

When a stronger acid (such as vinegar) is added to the baking soda, it replaces the weak acid. Since the weak acid is the same fizzy water in sodas, it fizzes in the volcano and makes tiny bubbles. The dishwashing soap helps these bubbles form a foam instead of just popping when they reach the surface.

If you like your volcanoes with real flames and sparks, you can use ammonium dichromate. A small pile of the compound can be lit with a match but should be done *with adult supervision, outside in a fire pit, barbecue, or fire-safe location*. It then burns with pretty red flames and orange sparks, and the ash expands, producing a typical volcano cone.

The ammonium dichromate is not actually burning. It is undergoing thermal decomposition. The atoms in the molecule are rearranging themselves to be in a lower energy state. If the compound is heated, it breaks down into green chromium oxide ash, water vapor, and nitrogen gas.

PROJECT: MAKING OXYGEN

Materials

Protective goggles
1 packet active dry yeast (available
  at grocery stores)
2-liter soda bottle, empty and clean
Hydrogen peroxide, 3 percent solution
  (available at drugstores and pharmacies)
Balloons
Candle
Bamboo skewer (optional)
Matches (optional)

Adult supervision required

You probably have everything you need to fill a balloon with pure oxygen. All it takes is some hydrogen peroxide from the medicine cabinet and some yeast from the kitchen.

All oxygen-breathing creatures make hydrogen peroxide as an inevitable byproduct of respiration. Since it can damage the cell if it is not destroyed, most cells have an enzyme called *catalase* that breaks hydrogen peroxide down into water and oxygen. That is why hydrogen

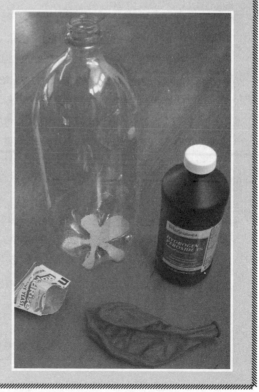

peroxide bubbles when you put it on a cut or scrape. Your own body has produced catalase, and that is breaking up the peroxide.

Yeast cells also breathe air and use the oxygen to burn sugar to get their energy. So they also produce hydrogen peroxide that they need to get rid of by using the catalase enzyme. So if you put some yeast in a bottle and pour in some hydrogen peroxide, you get bubbles of oxygen. The reaction is *exothermic*, meaning it generates heat, and you can feel the bottle get warm in your hand as the reaction takes place.

Pour the contents of a packet of active dry yeast into an empty two-liter soda bottle. Pour up to a couple inches of the hydrogen peroxide into the bottle. Three percent hydrogen peroxide, the kind you use for first aid, works fine. Be sure not to fill the bottle too high.

Place a balloon over the top of the bottle and watch it inflate as it fills with oxygen. The reason you had to be careful not to fill the bottle too high was so the bubbles won't flow over of the top and into the balloon. You may still have to shake or tap the bottle to prevent the bubbles from rising too high.

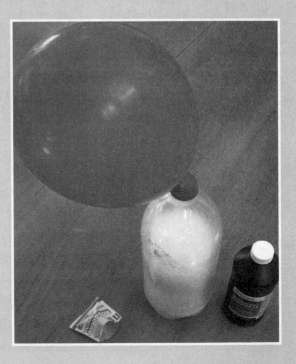

Once you have a balloon full of oxygen, you can start to have fun. For safety reasons, ***always wear protective goggles*** for this next part of the experiment.

First, see what happens when you blow up a balloon the normal way, using air from your lungs, and then aim it at a lit candle. Just like what happens on a birthday cake, the candle simply goes out. Now see what happens when you try to blow the candle out using the balloon full of pure oxygen.

See the video at http://youtu.be/ke6v-QYM4kA

The candle doesn't go out. Instead, it gets brighter. Look at how the camera adjusted to the extra brightness by making the rest of the picture dimmer.

You can use the same technique to make oxygen in a water glass, and then try to pop a bubble of oxygen with a hot coal on the end of a stick. (You can create one easily by lighting a bamboo skewer on fire then blowing it out, turning the end into a glowing-red coal.) When the bubble pops, a small explosion happens as the oxygen causes the hot coal to burst into flames. Of course, *you'll need protective goggles* for this experiment as well.

See the video at http://youtu.be/FPaDHie3tM8

6

Things That Stink

People wonder about the unusual things in life, but they wonder even more about the annoying things. Though they might never ask why a flower smells so nice, they almost always wonder what is making that awful smell.

Humans' main sense for detecting molecules is in their noses. Their tongues have only a few chemical sensors in them, and their other senses have even fewer. It is difficult to tell strong tea from vanilla extract by sight, touch, or sound. But the *nose* knows.

Why do things stink?

and . . .

Why do chemicals smell?

There are two mechanisms that cause odors that smell or stink.

Some things strongly irritate mucus membranes in your nose, eyes, and throat. Caustic chemicals such as ammonia, chlorine, and acid vapors stimulate pain sensors and make you jerk away from the odor.

But most smells are more subtle and are detected by special cells in your nose. An odor molecule may stimulate more than one cell, and different odors can be recognized by combinations of receptors. Each olfactory cell in the nose has a nerve that sends the information to the brain. Humans have about 40 million of these cells. Dogs have 50 times as many—about 2 billion. Humans have about 350 genes for odor receptors and can distinguish about 10,000 different odors.

If you are exposed to a particular smell for a while, you become used to it, and your body no longer detects it. The brain seems to be interested in new smells more than common smells, such as your own body odor. Women tend to have more sensitivity to odors than men do. Pregnancy enhances this effect. Humans' ability to detect odors decreases as they age.

Your ability to smell things helps you tell which foods are good to eat and which foods are rotten. It keeps you away from dangerous places that have high levels of bacteria or harmful vapors. Most of the things that smell bad are harmful to you or indicate that something may be harmful.

Why do skunks smell bad?

Skunks use their odor to defend themselves and keep predators away. Skunks spray a mixture of chemicals from special glands under the tail. These chemicals mostly contain molecules with a thiol group (a sulfur attached to a hydrogen).

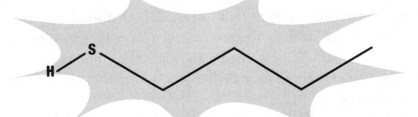

N-butyl mercaptan

These chemicals are known as *mercaptans*.

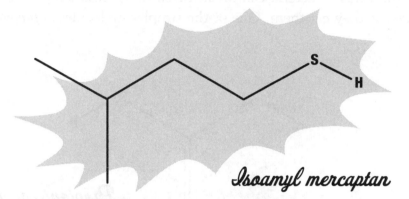

Isoamyl mercaptan

These are molecules that humans can sense when even one molecule is present among 10 billion air molecules.

A modification of these molecules is also present, where the thiol group has reacted with acetic acid to form what is called a *thioacetate*. These molecules have no smell but break down into the mercaptans when they get wet. This is why a dog that has been sprayed by a skunk smells worse when the air is humid.

Knowing that altering the thiol group removes the smell allows us to find remedies for skunk spray. If you oxidize the molecules with bleach, they lose their aroma. This is fine for washing clothes, but to wash a pet, you need something milder than chlorine bleach.

Hydrogen peroxide will work, but only if it is in an alkaline solution. So if you wash the dog in a mixture of baking soda and peroxide, much of the odor goes away. Repeating the wash helps, as does a final wash with a scented shampoo.

What is the chemical reaction that makes your feet smell?

Your feet sweat, just like the rest of you does. Sweat itself is normally odorless, but it contains nutrients for bacteria and provides a nice warm, moist place for them to live.

Sweat contains amino acids and proteins (which are made of amino acids). Bacteria can break these down into simpler molecules as they eat them. One of the simpler molecules is *propionic acid*.

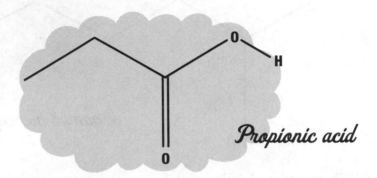

Propionic acid

Propionic acid has the same structure as the acetic acid in vinegar, except it has an extra carbon atom added on the left side. It has a strong vinegary odor.

Another similar breakdown product of amino acids by bacteria is *isovaleric acid*. It also has a strong smell, and it is one of the molecules bacteria produce when they break down amino acids during the manufacture of cheese. This molecule is one of the main contributors to the aroma of cheese.

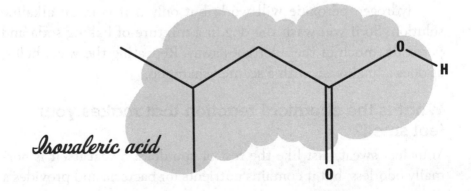

Isovaleric acid

So if your socks smell faintly of vinegar or cheese, you can blame the bacteria we use to make vinegar and cheese. They are at work in your shoes.

What is the chemical reaction that makes your breath smell?

When is your tongue like your socks? When it harbors bacteria that make bad smells.

Almost all of the odor in bad breath (called *halitosis* by doctors) comes from your tongue. Some may come from the gums if you have gum disease. Some comes from the rest of the mouth or the throat, nose, or stomach, but by far the most fertile ground for breeding halitosis bacteria is the broad top surface of the tongue.

The top of your tongue has many little crevices that bacteria can live in. Most of the bacteria that cause bad breath are *anaerobes*, bacteria that grow best without air. As you sleep, they grow undisturbed, and you wake up with morning breath.

As the bacteria digest food particles and dead skin cells on the tongue, they create waste products that include the hydrogen sulfide that gives rotten eggs their odor, the methyl mercaptan that is present in skunk scent, and other sulfur-containing small, volatile molecules that result from the breakdown of sulfur-containing proteins.

Amino acids that don't contain sulfur also break down into smelly molecules. Tryptophan breaks down into *indole*. It is one of the molecules that gives fecal matter—animal droppings—its odor.

Another product of tryptophan breakdown is *skatole*, which is just indole with an extra methyl group added. It is also found in feces and contributes to that characteristic odor.

So please do us all a favor: brush the top of your tongue in the morning when you brush your teeth.

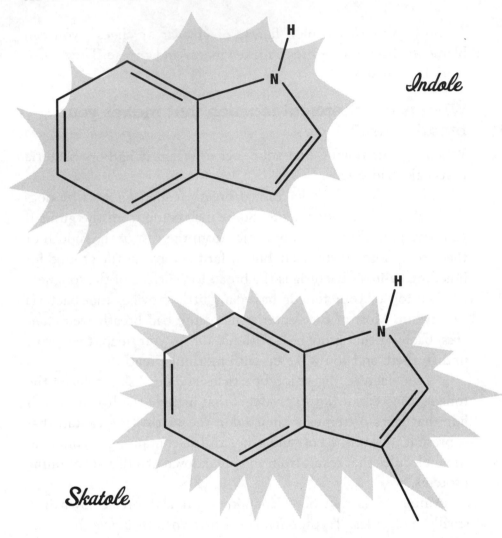

Indole

Skatole

Why does nail polish smell so strong?

Nail polish contains several ingredients that give it its strong odor. Some of those ingredients are the solvents used to keep the plastic liquid until it dries on your toenails. Butyl acetate, ethyl acetate, and toluene are examples. Butyl acetate gives bananas their smell and is also used to flavor candies.

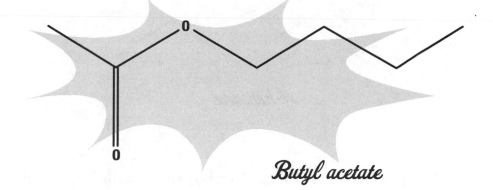

Butyl acetate

Ethyl acetate is similar ester that smells like pears. When these two molecules are present in huge amounts, they can have a very strong odor.

Toluene is derived from petroleum and gives paint thinner its characteristic smell. It is also used as the fluid that fuels some cigarette lighters.

Nail polish may also include camphor, a strong-smelling molecule that is used to keep the plastic flexible. Camphor is now made synthetically, but it was originally found in the camphor laurel tree that grows in China and Borneo. It is sometimes used as a moth repellant (the tree probably produced it as an insecticide). It gives Vicks VapoRub its strong scent.

Nail polish remover also has an interesting smell. It is mostly acetone, a strong organic solvent that is good at dissolving many plastics, glues, and paints.

Why do some glues smell strong?

There are several types of glues. Glues that use a plastic or rubber dissolved in a petroleum-based solvent will smell like the solvent. For example, rubber cement is latex rubber dissolved in n-heptane.

N-heptane

N-heptane is just a chain of 7 carbon atoms, with 2 hydrogen atoms attached to each carbon and another hydrogen at each end. It is a component of gasoline and smells like it.

Model airplane cement uses toluene as a solvent. It also has a characteristic odor.

Some glues, like epoxy, come in two parts, which react together to form a new molecule. Each part contains some volatile molecules that have characteristic odors, but as they cure they can also emit new molecules with different odors.

Silicone rubber adhesives combine with the moisture in the air to cure, and in the curing process they release lactic acid, which has a sharp, eye-stinging odor.

What chemicals make perfume?

There are thousands of chemicals that are used in perfumes. But many of them can be grouped according to their chemical properties.

One such group is esters. An ester is what you get when you let an alcohol react with certain types of acids (acids that contain oxygen). Esters are the main thing you smell when you sniff fruits and flowers.

The scent of pineapple, for example, is largely due to the molecules allyl hexanoate, butyl butyrate, ethyl butyrate, methyl butyrate, pentyl butyrate, and pentyl hexanoate.

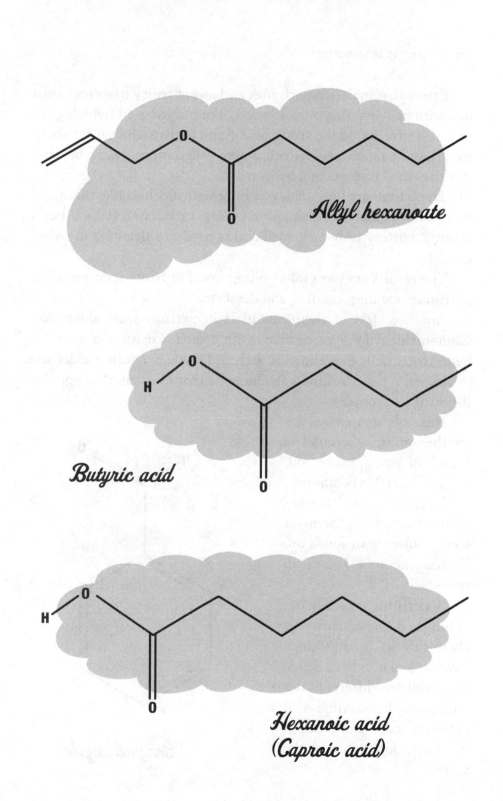

Allyl hexanoate

Butyric acid

Hexanoic acid
(Caproic acid)

Esters that make up perfumes and sweet fruity flavorings start out with bad-smelling organic acids, like butyric acid (which gives rancid butter its odor), acetic acid (which gives vinegar its sharp smell), or hexanoic acid, which is also called caproic acid, because it is the smell of goats in a barnyard.

These foul-smelling acids combine with alcohols like methanol or ethanol (which have almost no odor) or butanol (which has a creamy, buttery taste and smell and is used as a flavoring in baked goods).

The results are pleasant-smelling floral or fruity scents used in perfumes, candies, candles, and desserts.

Another class of chemicals used in perfumes are aldehydes. Cinnamaldehyde gives cinnamon its aroma. Furfural is an aldehyde that smells like almonds. Benzaldehyde is another aldehyde in almond scent. Vanillin is an aldehyde that gives another popular flavoring its aroma.

Alcohols themselves are another group. Geraniol is found in roses, lemon oil, and (of course) in geraniums.

Ketones are another group. Civetone is the main scent molecule in musk oil. Damascone is a ketone in rose scent.

A perfume typically has a hundred or so different chemicals in it, and some have several hundred. There are about ten different odor molecules in jasmine and between three and a dozen in a rose, depending on the variety.

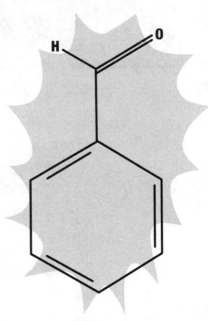

Benzaldehyde

Why do some plants smell and others don't?

Plants make molecules that have aromas for several reasons. Some of the molecules are used by the plant to attract insects for pollination. Other molecules are there to repel insects that might otherwise dine on the plant.

Sometimes a plant has an odor simply because some of the molecules in it are volatile and make their way through the air to your nose. Pine scents contain many light molecules that float through the air easily. Some of these are insecticide molecules, and our noses are pretty good at detecting molecules that might be toxic.

The smell of freshly cut grass is due in part to molecules the plant gives off when under attack by insects. These "green leaf volatiles" attract predatory insects that eat the bugs that are eating the grass. In order to do their job, they have to travel through the air and land on the scent-detecting cells on the antennae of the predatory bugs. But we can smell them too.

Some of the molecules in cut grass are antimicrobials, and they are part of the plant's reaction to injury. They are there to kill bacteria and fungus. Our noses are sensitive to molecules that are active enough to kill germs.

7

Color

People use their sense of sight more than any other sense. A dog may experience the world mostly through its nose, and a bat through its ears, but most humans depend on sight.

A black and white world would seem quite dull to us. We would see shapes and detect movement, both very important things, but we evolved color vision because it gives us many advantages, telling us what is ripe, what is rotten, and what is hiding in the grass.

Why are there so many colors in the world?

There are actually only three colors that we can see. Our eyes contain color-sensing cells called *cones*. There are three types, and they each can sense one color. The colors are red, green, and blue.

But the cones in your eyes respond rather broadly to the light that comes in, so that some red light will also stimulate the green cones, and to a lesser extent the blue cones. Some blue light will stimulate the green cones, and the red cones a little bit less. And some green light will stimulate the blue and red cones.

As a result, colors of light that lie in between the colors that the cones receive best will stimulate two or more cones at the same time. You see light that stimulates red and green cones at the same time as yellow. Violet light stimulates the blue and the red cones.

How do you make a fluorescent light?

You have seen toys that glow in the dark, and you have seen fluorescent colors in clothing and highlighting markers that seem to glow even when it isn't dark. These objects glow because they contain compounds called *phosphors*.

A phosphor absorbs light of one color, and that energy is stored in the molecule (scientists say that the molecule is *excited*), and a little bit later the energy is released again as light and heat. Since some of the energy is lost as heat, the light that comes out has less energy than the light that went in. Light with less energy is redder in color.

So, to make a fluorescent light, you want to start with light that has a lot of energy (light that has a shorter wavelength). If light has a lot of energy, it will move so far in the blue direction that it goes past violet into the ultraviolet, which we cannot see.

A fluorescent bulb is a tube of glass that has a little bit of mercury in it and very little else (almost a vacuum). When electricity is put into the mercury vapor, the mercury gets excited and emits ultraviolet light, as well as some green and blue light and a little bit of red.

Now, if the inside of the tube is coated with glow-in-the-dark phosphors that absorb the ultraviolet light, they will emit exactly the colors we want. Little bits of each color of phosphor can added to tune the light to be any shade of white (or any other color) desired. The tube can simulate sunlight or get a bluer or redder light to suit the mood.

Since the mercury vapor emits mostly light and very little heat, compared to heating up a tungsten filament until it glows white hot, fluorescent lights use less energy than incandescent lights of the same brightness.

How do people make different nail polish colors?

Since nail polish is a cosmetic, the pigments and dyes are selected from the list of D&C colors regulated by governments. These colors were discussed earlier in the question about the colors in shampoo (page 31).

The pigments in nail polish are generally dissolved with a film-forming plastic in a solvent. A typical film-forming plastic used is the explosive nitrocellulose, one of the ingredients in smokeless gunpowder. This is dissolved in a relatively safe solvent, such as ethyl acetate or butyl acetate (or both) and sometimes isopropanol.

To make the colors opaque, pigments such as titanium dioxide may be added. Thickeners such as stearalkonium bentonite (a type of clay) are also added. To get pearlescent effects, flakes of fish scales, tiny flakes of aluminum, or even minute flakes of stainless steel can be added. These give metallic sheen to the nail polish. Platelets of mica can also be used to give a shiny effect.

Why are so many powders white?

and . . .

Why is milk white?

and . . .

Why are clouds white?

All of these things are white because the light that hits them is scattered by all the tiny particles or droplets in them. When light hits a tiny particle or droplet of water or fat, it bounces off. All colors bounce off equally. When we see something that emits or reflects all colors at the same time, it appears white.

The fat droplets that make milk white come in a variety of sizes but group into three main diameters: 120 nanometers, 400 nanometers, and 1,500 nanometers. Visible light waves range from 400 nanometers to 800 nanometers, so the size of the fat droplets is just about the size of a wavelength of visible light.

The water droplets in clouds range from 6,000 to 14,000 nanometers. This is still much too small to see, especially when the clouds are a mile above you, so we see what looks like a solid object.

If particles are too small, a powder does not look white, especially when it is in a liquid. This is why the same chemical, titanium dioxide, can be a bright white in paint but invisible in sunscreen if the particles are smaller than a wavelength of visible light.

Why is the sky blue?

The sky is actually a little bit on the violet side. It only looks blue because your eyes are much more sensitive to blue light than to violet light.

When white light from the sun travels through clear air, it hits the molecules of nitrogen and oxygen and gets scattered a little bit, so it travels in a slightly different direction. Since there are miles of air between you and the sun, the light will scatter many times.

But how much the light is scattered depends on the color. Blue light is scattered about 10 times more than red light. This is called *Rayleigh scattering*, after the man who worked out the math. Violet light is the light that is scattered the most out of all the light your eyes can see. This is why the sun looks yellow to you: white light from the sun will look yellow if you remove the violet light by scattering it away.

But your eyes are not very sensitive to violet light. They are very sensitive to blue light. They are also sensitive to green light and red light. A little bit of the violet light excites the red light sensing cones in your eyes, which is why violet looks like blue with a little red in it. It is also why the sky looks light blue instead of deep blue.

When the sun is near the horizon, there is more air between it and your eyes. The light near the sun has more red and yellow because light that is scattered only one or two times does not change direction much. There is also more dust and smog, which scatter more red and yellow light. So sunsets are red, yellow, orange, and pink.

Why is water clear?

Water is clear because nothing in it reflects light.

You can see things because light from them gets into your eyes. If something has nothing in it to bend or bounce light, you don't see it. This is why air and glass are both clear.

There are times when you can see these things. If the air has dust in it, you see the dust. Or if the air in one place is hotter or colder than in another place, you can see the effect of the difference because it bends the light, and things on the other side look distorted or appear to move.

If glass is perfectly clean, you might not know it is there and walk into it. But if the glass is not smooth and flat, you can see how it distorts things you see through it, and you can tell where it is. If the water or glass has a dye in it that absorbs some color of light, then you see all the colors but that one, and you know the glass is there. If the glass absorbs yellow light, it will look blue.

Water and most glasses actually do absorb red and yellow light more than they do blue, so if there is enough water or glass, it looks blue.

Why is grass green?

Grass is green because you water the lawn. Grasses that have evolved to tolerate drought have less chlorophyll than grasses in wetter environments. Chlorophyll (the pigment that absorbs red and blue light to make sugar from water and carbon dioxide) reflects green light, but in absorbing the other colors, it warms up.

If there isn't enough water, the blades of grass close up the little holes, called *stomata*, where water evaporates to cool the leaves. If there is not enough water, the plant produces less of the chlorophyll molecule and can survive the heat better.

In the summer, many grasses (especially in arid or semi-arid areas) lose their chlorophyll altogether. They turn the color of straw. In some the chlorophyll is lost because the sunlight breaks it down, and the plant does not replace it. In others, the plant actively removes the chlorophyll and stores the valuable materials in another part of the plant. In some annual grasses, that part is the seeds.

How do you make colored milk?

We can color the milk by either adding something or taking something away. The white color of milk is caused by particles and droplets in the milk that reflect (scatter) the light that hits them. If you remove the droplets of fat from whole milk, it takes on the slightly bluish tint of nonfat milk.

If you add brown powdered cocoa, the cocoa particles absorb a good deal of the light that hits them, but they reflect enough red and yellow to appear brown. The milk adds white reflections, so the result is a lighter shade of brown than that of the original cocoa powder.

You can make pink milk by adding red food coloring. The red dye absorbs green and blue light. The milk adds white, giving us pink.

Because of the effect the droplets of fat have on the light, it is hard to get deep, dark colors when adding dyes to milk. Even adding India ink only makes a gray color.

What makes disappearing ink disappear?

Carbon dioxide. A common type of disappearing ink is based on an acid-base indicator called *thymolphthalein*. This is a molecule that absorbs visible light when it is in an alkaline solution and becomes colorless in a neutral or acidic solution.

To turn it into a blue ink, sodium hydroxide (lye), a strong alkali, is added. As long as the solution is basic (alkaline), it will be blue. But if you allow the ink to soak into paper or cloth, so that there is a lot of surface area in contact with the air, it will absorb carbon dioxide from the air. Carbon dioxide mixes with water to form carbonic acid (the bubbly ingredient in soda pop). The acid neutralizes the lye, forming sodium carbonate (washing soda). The neutral solution is no longer blue, but colorless.

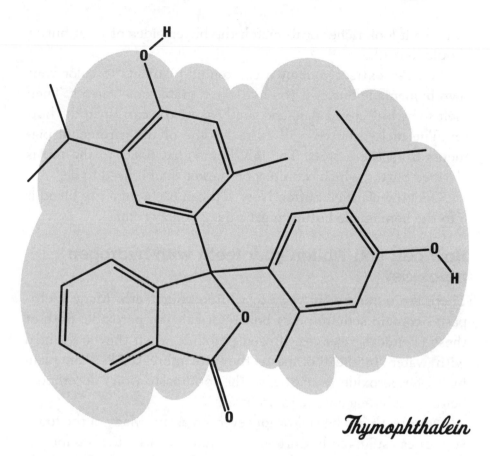

Thymophthalein

You can make it blue again by adding an alkali, such as baking soda or ammonia (or more lye).

Why is butter yellow?

Some milk contains a lot of carotenoid pigments in the butterfat. When the butterfat is skimmed off and churned into butter, the butter is yellow.

You make homemade butter by shaking a jar full of heavy whipping cream (or overwhipping your cream), but it is seldom as dark a yellow color as the butter you buy in the store. This is because commercial butter often has carotenoid pigments added to make it look richer or to match the buyer's idea of what butter should look like.

You can extract your own carotenoid pigments to color your own homemade butter if you like. First, grate some carrots. Then melt some butter in a pan, and gently sauté the carrots in the butter. The melted butter will extract some of the carotenoid pigments from the carrots. The oily liquid that floats to the top is clarified butter, which is quite a bit darker than it used to be.

Cool the clarified butter. Now you can use a mixer to blend it into the homemade butter to get a deep yellow color.

How can you whiten your teeth with hydrogen peroxide?

There are a number of ways to whiten your teeth. Many toothpastes contain sodium percarbonate or calcium peroxide. Both of these chemicals release hydrogen peroxide when they are mixed with water. In the toothpaste they are more stable than plain hydrogen peroxide would be, so the toothpaste won't decompose before you have a chance to use it.

Your teeth can be yellow for several reasons. Many of the foods you eat can stain teeth. Coffee, tea, and tobacco are famous for yellowing teeth, but many other foods also have this ability. Peroxide toothpastes, or a rinse of 3 percent hydrogen peroxide, can help remove most of the stains. Peroxide bleaches the yellow by oxidizing the stain molecules so that they no longer absorb light.

Bacteria that live in your mouth make a protein film on the teeth called a biofilm. This is easily stained and may be slightly yellow all by itself. Peroxide bleaches the stain molecules, but it also breaks up the protein film so you can brush it away.

If you have been brushing your teeth for many years, the white enamel on the outside of the tooth may get thin enough that the yellow dentin inside the tooth shows through. Peroxide can penetrate into the dentin and bleach the yellow to a whiter color.

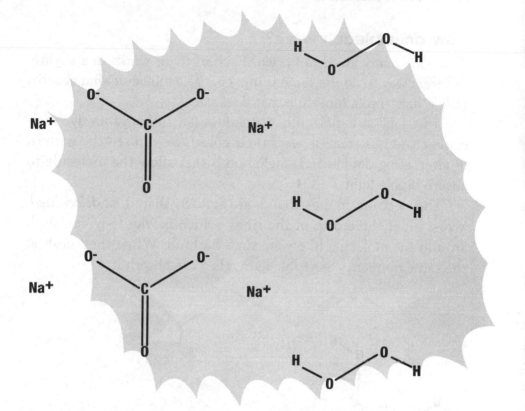

Sodium percarbonate

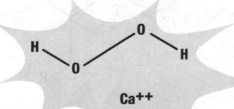

Calcium peroxide

How does bleach work?

There are many kinds of bleach. Each of them works in a slightly different way to do the same thing: change a molecule that absorbs visible light into a molecule that does not.

If we look at a molecule of cyanidin (an anthocyanin dye molecule that gives some flowers their color), we can see the pattern of alternating double and single bonds that allow the molecule to absorb visible light.

The electrons in these bonds are actually shared, or *delocalized*, across all of the atoms in the rings, which is why they can slosh around the molecule like water in a bathtub. When they slosh at the same frequency as visible light, they can absorb it.

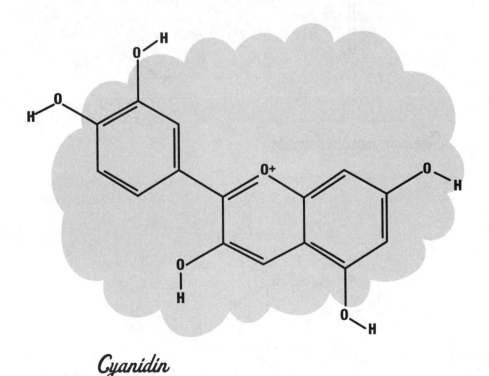

Cyanidin

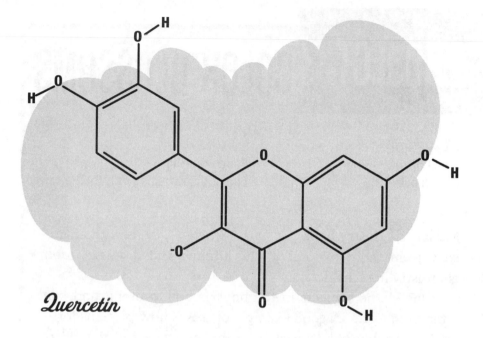

Quercetin

Chlorine bleach and hydrogen peroxide both provide oxygen atoms that can combine with the molecule to change the loops so they no longer have delocalized electrons to slosh around.

Quercetin is a molecule in which oxygen atoms have been added to cyanidin. The ring in the middle no longer has delocalized electrons, and the molecule is colorless.

Other chemicals can also bleach dye molecules such as cyanidin. Sulfur dioxide and sulfites can add SO_2 groups to the molecule that also steal electrons from the center ring, causing the molecule to become colorless.

PROJECT: COLOR BLOSSOMS

Materials

Small bowl
Whole milk

Food coloring
Liquid dishwashing detergent

My last chemistry book, *Culinary Reactions*, deals with chemistry from the viewpoint of the kitchen and discusses food chemistry in some detail.

One of the subjects in the book is how proteins and fats interact in water. A good example of this is how proteins form around droplets of butterfat in cream and whole milk, stabilizing the emulsion of fat in water.

You can destabilize the emulsion by adding something that combines with fat and water better than the proteins do. Soaps and detergents do exactly that, and you can demonstrate their effect with a very colorful display.

In the photo on the next page, I started off with a bowl of whole milk (nonfat milk won't work), to which I added some drops of food coloring. Notice that the drops are just sitting there, not mixing much at all with the milk.

Next I added a drop of dishwashing detergent.

The colors exploded, racing away from the detergent. But they didn't stop. They continued to mix and swirl around the bowl for more than a minute. They flowed and folded and moved around, quite unlike what they were doing before I added the detergent.

What happened is that the detergent interacted with the oil, the water, and the proteins in the milk. The detergent had molecules on which one end liked to stay in water and the

See the video at http://youtu.be/SwsCQtipAus

other end liked to stay in fats and oils. Many of the proteins in the milk also had parts that were water-loving (*hydrophilic*) and other parts that were water-avoiding (*hydrophobic*).

The detergent moved in to replace the proteins at the interface between the butterfat and the water. But the detergent also attached to the proteins at their water-loving and water-avoiding parts, and this changed the shapes of the proteins and changed how the proteins attached to one another.

All of this rearranging can take some time—up to several minutes—to complete. As the molecules rearranged, they pushed the water and the food coloring around, causing them to stir up into beautiful blossoms of color.

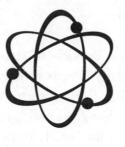

8

Chemistry in the World

The whole world is made of atoms, and those atoms react with one another to create the molecules that make up everything we see. What things are made of and how they come to be made is the province of chemistry.

Some chemical reactions are interesting because of the hint of danger. I keep a Dewar of liquid nitrogen here in the lab, and Alexa loves to play with it when she comes over, freezing whipped cream so that she can chew it and make fog come out of her mouth like a dragon. She has heard of things like electrons and gluons and biochemistry, but until she asked the questions, she had no idea why they might be important.

Why is there salt in the ocean?

Because salt dissolves easily in water. Water in the oceans evaporates into the air, leaving solids like salt behind. The water vapor then rises and cools until it falls as rain. If the nearly pure water in the rain falls on land, it dissolves some of the dirt it falls on. Rain that has dissolved carbon dioxide in it is slightly acidic, and the acid helps dissolve the dirt. Dirt is mostly silica, so about 15 percent of the dissolved solids in river water turns out to be dissolved silica—silicon dioxide, what glass and quartz is made of.

Many things dissolve more easily than silica. Gypsum (calcium sulfate), for example, and chalk (calcium carbonate), each dissolve in slightly acidic water, adding calcium, sulfate, carbonate, and bicarbonate ions to the water. But sodium and chlorine ions are even more soluble. There is just much more of the other ions in dirt than there is salt. So the solids in river water are mostly bicarbonate ions (from the carbon dioxide in the air), calcium, silica, sulfate, chloride, sodium, and magnesium, in that order.

But when the river water gets to the sea, the organisms in the ocean start to remove ions from the water to build their shells. Diatoms in plankton remove silica. Other plankton and shellfish remove calcium and bicarbonate ions to make shells and coral reefs.

As the water evaporates and concentrates the ions, the less soluble ones precipitate out of the water and fall to the bottom of the ocean. Calcium carbonate, calcium sulfate, and magnesium sulfate form deposits on the sea floor. But no living organism builds its house out of salt, and very little salt gets locked up in the mud. Therefore, ocean water ends up being mostly salt water, with a number of other molecules in it, but in much smaller amounts.

What happens when you play with liquid nitrogen?

Liquid nitrogen boils off into the air, where it came from, at room temperature.

Liquid nitrogen is made by compressing and cooling air. Air is mostly nitrogen. The oxygen in the air becomes a liquid at a higher temperature than nitrogen, so it liquefies first and boils off last, when air is liquefied. When the gases that liquefy first are removed, almost pure nitrogen is left.

Liquid nitrogen boils at −320° Fahrenheit. So having a bowl of liquid nitrogen in your kitchen is similar to having a bowl of water in an oven at 600° F. The water would boil away. But as long as there was water left in the bowl, the water itself would still only be at a temperature of 212° F—the boiling point.

The same thing happens with liquid nitrogen. As long as there is liquid in the bowl, it cannot get hotter than the boiling point. So anything we put in the liquid will be cooled to the boiling point of the liquid.

When a rose is put into liquid nitrogen, the liquid vigorously boils around the rose, since the rose is 400° F hotter than the liquid's boiling point. The rose transfers its heat to the nitrogen until they are both at the same temperature: −320° F.

At that temperature, the water in the rose petals is frozen solid. The petals become as brittle as thin sheets of glass. If the rose is then dropped onto a table before the air can melt the ice, the rose will shatter into hundreds of tiny shards. But you have to act quickly—the air is 400° F hotter than the rose petals and can melt the ice quickly.

Why do some chemicals stain your hands?

Sometimes it is just because they are colored chemicals. If you rub your hands in food coloring, on grass, or on wet paint, the molecules that make these things absorb light will be left on your hands.

Some molecules are better at sticking to skin than others. You can rub your hands in dark yellow egg yolk, but the dark substance is easy to wipe off with a paper towel. It does not leave a stain. The molecules that make egg yolk yellow are large and don't attach themselves to the skin.

Food coloring, on the other hand, is made from very small molecules that can get into the very small crevices and pores in the skin, and they can even react with the skin itself, forming chemical bonds that make them stick tightly there. To wash them off, you need lots of water to help them dissolve and be carried away, but you may also need to scrub off the top layer of dead skin cells to which the dye has bonded.

Some chemicals react with the skin and change its color. Skin can be burned or bleached with strong oxidizers. Some other chemicals react with the skin and themselves change color. Potassium permanganate ($KMnO_4$) will oxidize (burn) the skin and make manganese dioxide, which stains the skin brown. Silver nitrate will react with the skin and the salt on the skin to form silver chloride, which will then break down in strong light to form tiny particles of silver. These silver particles stay stuck in the skin and look black. As the skin grows and the cells die and are scrubbed off, the stain gradually goes away.

Nitric acid reacts with (burns) the skin, creating a yellow or brown stain. It is particularly dangerous because the nerves in the skin do not react to it, so you may not realize you are getting burned.

What happens when you put your hand in an acid?

That will depend on the acid and on how much the acid is diluted. There are strong acids and weak acids. There are oxidizing acids and non-oxidizing acids. In general, skin reacts to strong acids and oxidizing acids.

People handle weak acids all the time. Carbonated water is a weak acid. So is the citric acid that makes orange juice taste sour. Some weak acids, like the acetic acid in vinegar, can attack skin if they are concentrated. In vinegar, the acetic acid is highly diluted, so you can even drink it. Some strong acids, like hydrochloric acid, don't react much with skin if they are diluted well. Your stomach produces hydrochloric acid, and the lining of the stomach is protected from it by a layer of mucus. Even so, the hydrochloric acid in the stomach is often less acidic than the typical carbonated beverage, because it is diluted with water.

Concentrated strong acids and diluted oxidizing acids can burn skin. The acids react with the proteins in skin and break them down, so they can no longer act as a barrier. The acid can then continue to react with tissues, killing cells. Living tissue can only function within a narrow range of acidity, and outside of that range the cells die.

Sulfuric acid is not only a strong acid, but it reacts with the water in your skin so strongly that it will create blisters. This is not because of its acidity but because of its dehydrating ability.

You can protect your hands from strong acids by wearing gloves made of materials the acid cannot attack. With many acids the fumes are also dangerous, so you should also make sure that you have plenty of ventilation. The fumes can attack the lining of your nose, throat, and lungs, as well as your eyes. Always wear eye protection when working with acids and bases.

What happens when you put a leaf in an acid?

That will depend on the acid. Leaves are protected by several barriers, such as a wax coating, and thick cell walls made of lignin, cellulose, and pectin, none of which react very much with most acids. But they do eventually react, if slowly. That is why special acid-free paper is used for artwork and archival documents. Paper is mostly cellulose, and acid will eventually make it brittle and yellow.

Strong acids like sulfuric and nitric acid will dissolve a leaf. The thinnest parts of the leaf will dissolve first, since there is less material there. The result is a lacy, delicate web of the ribs of the leaf that give it strength and structure. You could then neutralize the acid to prevent further corrosive action and preserve the lacy leaf.

Living leaves have pores in them (called *stomata*) that allow them to breathe. If acids get in these pores, it can kill the cells inside the leaf.

Dead leaves have less protective wax on them, and they can absorb water and acids more easily. The dried leaves are thus more prone to attack by acid and will deteriorate faster than a freshly picked green leaf.

What do electrons do?

Electrons jump away from one another. That one fact explains most of electricity. If you push more electrons into a wire, they all push against one another and will move toward the place where there is the least pressure. We call that pressure *voltage*. A *current* is simply how many electrons are moving past a particular point in a second. *Electrical power* is how much pressure there is, multiplied by the amount of current.

In chemistry, electrons are what hold molecules together. Electrons are attracted to the positive charges at the center of atoms, but only specific numbers of electrons can fit in each energy-level shell around the nucleus.

If an atom has an empty spot in an energy level, and another atom has an electron in an otherwise empty energy level, that lone electron can fall into the empty space in the other atom's shell, and the two atoms will stick together, because both nuclei will be pulling on that one electron.

This also works if there is more than one empty slot or more than one extra electron. The electrons will fall into the energy level as close to a nucleus as possible, no matter which atom it is in. So an oxygen atom, which has two empty slots in its shell, can take the lone electron from two hydrogen atoms and make a molecule of water. By sharing electrons in this way, the electrons can fall into the lowest energy level, closest to the nucleus.

In metals, the outer energy shells of the atoms merge into one big, empty slot, and the outer electrons can move around freely. In atoms like chlorine, the empty slot is so close to the nucleus that the electron spends most of its time near the chlorine atom and little time around the atom it came from (for example, the sodium atom in a molecule of salt). This allows the molecule to dissolve easily in water, leaving a positive sodium ion and a negative chloride ion.

How do we get electricity?

Electricity is mostly mechanically produced. Mechanical energy is turned into electrical energy in machines called *generators*.

Electricity and magnetism are two sides of the same thing. Moving electrons create magnetic fields. Moving magnetic fields cause electrons to move. In a generator, a magnetic field is made to move near copper wires. The electrons in the wires begin to move, and the moving electrons are what we call electricity.

Moving electrons can heat up wires as they move through them. Electric stoves and incandescent lights work by heating up wires this way. Since moving electrons create magnetic fields, and magnets can attract one another, we can make electric motors to power our gadgets around the house.

The electricity that comes out of the plug in your house is made by a generator, but there are other ways to make electricity. It can be made directly from heat in a simple device called a *thermocouple*. Twist together two different kinds of wire, such as copper wire and iron wire, and when you get the twisted part hot, it makes electrons move.

Electricity can also be made from light using solar cells or from pressure by using a piezoelectric ceramic, such as those in electric lighters. Electricity can be made by moving electrons on an insulator past some sharp wires in a Van de Graaff generator or chemically by building a battery.

How do you use chemistry to make a battery?

Metals are used to make a battery. Metals have a convenient property called *conduction*, in which the electrons in the metal are not bound to just one atom at a time as in other materials but are free to wander from atom to atom. This allows the metals to conduct electricity, because electricity is just charged particles moving through something like a wire.

Many other things can also conduct electricity. For example, hydrochloric acid is a good conductor. When hydrogen chloride (HCl) dissolves in water, it breaks up into hydrogen ions (H^+) and chloride ions (Cl^-). These electrically charged particles can move through the water. Moving charged particles is electricity.

If you put a strip of aluminum and a strip of copper into the same acid and then the two metal strips are connected to a meter, you can watch electricity being created. Copper holds on to electrons more tightly than aluminum does. Electrons start to move from the aluminum, through the meter, to the copper.

This leaves the aluminum with a positive charge. It attracts the negative chloride ions to it, through the water. The chloride ions attract positive aluminum ions away from the metal strip and into the water, where they form an aluminum chloride solution.

At the copper strip, the extra electrons attract the hydrogen ions in the solution to migrate toward the copper. When they get there, they can steal the electrons to become hydrogen gas. The hydrogen gas bubbles up out of the solution. This keeps up until there is no more aluminum left on the aluminum strip. All the electrons flowing from the aluminum to the copper have been moving the needle of the meter, showing us that electricity has been produced.

How do solar panels work?

In some ways, solar panels work like batteries and thermocouples. Two dissimilar conductors are placed together, and electrons move from the one that holds them loosely to the one that holds them tighter.

There are many types of solar cell materials, and not all of them work in the same way. In the simplest ones, a photon of light knocks an electron off a metal, and that electron flies off to another conductor and then goes through a circuit to get back to the original metal plate.

But most solar cells these days use semiconductor materials in what is called a *p-n junction*. In a silicon solar cell, the two sides of the p-n junction are made of silicon. A small amount of phosphorus is added to one side to make the n material. A small amount of boron is added to the other side to make the p material.

Phosphorus has one more outer electron than silicon does. Boron has one less. The electron from the phosphorus becomes a conduction electron, allowing electric current to flow in the material. In the p material, the missing electron from the boron creates a "hole." An electron from silicon can move into the hole, leaving another hole behind. In this way, the holes can appear to move around.

When the p and n materials are put together to form a p-n junction, the extra phosphorus electrons in the n material are attracted to the holes left by the boron in the p material. This creates a *voltage gradient* in the cell—a gradual change in the voltage that causes electrons to slide down it. (Think of it like a playground slide, which is a gravity gradient that causes *you* to slide down it.)

When a photon of light hits the semiconductor, an electron is excited and becomes a conduction electron. It moves along the voltage gradient from the negative side of the cell to the positive side. The hole it created when it left the silicon atom moves toward the positive side, just as a bubble of air in water floats to the surface.

When the solar cell is connected to a meter or to a light bulb, the electrons can flow through the wires to get back to the other side of the p-n junction, filling in the holes, so the whole process can start over again.

How does a Van de Graaff generator work?

A Van de Graaff generator is a device for making very high-voltage electricity. It usually has a metal sphere situated above a plastic tube. Inside the tube is a rubber band that is made to move by a motor. A wire brush is attached to the metal sphere and almost touches the rubber band. Another wire brush almost touches the rubber band at the bottom.

Rubber is an insulator, so electrons on it cannot easily move around. This means that when a few extra electrons are added or a few are taken away, the negative or positive charge remains in that place on the rubber band.

The rubber is attached at the top to a pulley made of glass, Teflon, or some other material. As the rubber leaves the glass pulley, electrons are transferred from the glass to the rubber, because rubber holds electrons more tightly than glass does.

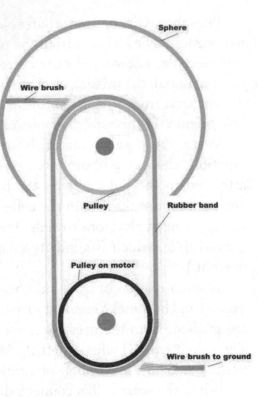

The glass is now positively charged. It pulls electrons from the wire brush at the top. This leaves the metal sphere with a positive charge. The positive charges repel one another and flow to the outside of the sphere, leaving the inside uncharged, so it can always lose electrons.

As the rubber band moves around, the negatively charged rubber is moved down next to the bottom wire brush. The electrons jump onto air molecules and then onto the wire, always trying to get away from one another.

The rubber is now neutral and is brought around to the glass pulley to start the whole process over again. The top sphere becomes more positively charged with each revolution of the rubber band. The electrons leave by the bottom wire, where they build up on any surface they are connected to. Eventually, the charge separation (voltage) is so high that electrons are stolen from the air, and the air becomes conductive. A big spark conducts electrons to the sphere, and the voltage drops again.

Then the whole process starts over.

What does water have to do with chemistry?

Most of chemistry deals with water, and water has been called the "universal solvent." Both of these things have to do with water's ability to form *hydrogen bonds*.

These bonds are the reason sodium chloride can dissolve easily in water. In a molecule of water, the oxygen atom attracts the electrons from the hydrogens so strongly that they stay around the oxygen atom most of the time and only sometimes swing back around to the hydrogen atoms. This makes the oxygen atom slightly negative and leaves the hydrogen atoms slightly positive. The positive hydrogen atoms on the water molecule attract the negative chloride ions in the salt. The negative oxygen atom in the water molecule attracts the positive sodium ion in the salt. This attraction competes with the attraction of the sodium and chlorine for each other and has the effect of weakening their attraction. If there is enough heat energy to jostle the atoms around, the salt will dissolve in the water.

More generally, a hydrogen bond is the attraction of the positive hydrogen nucleus to negative ions or negative parts of other molecules. Hydrogen bonds also make the water molecules attract *one another*, so water is a liquid at room temperature. Without hydrogen bonds, it would be a gas, like it is when it is hot enough that the motion of the molecules overcomes the hydrogen bonds.

Hydrogen bonds are what make ice take up more room than liquid water, so ice floats. When water freezes, hydrogen bonds lock the molecules into place, and the shape of the water molecule forces them into hexagons that take up more room than the randomly moving water molecules in liquid water. Hydrogen bonds are also very important in shaping proteins in living things, and water affects how the proteins work.

What are atoms?

An atom is the smallest thing a chemical element can be divided into. An atom can be broken down into smaller parts, but then it would no longer be the same chemical element.

An atom is made up of a nucleus around which are some number of electrons. The nucleus is made up of a number of protons, whose positive charges attract a similar number of electrons, which have negative charges. The number of protons an atom has is its atomic number and determines what chemical element the atom is.

Hydrogen is an element with a single proton. It attracts a single electron. That electron can be taken away, leaving a hydrogen ion. An ion is an atom that is either missing one or more electrons or which has one or more extra electrons.

Hydrogen can also have one or two neutrons in the nucleus, along with the proton. Neutrons don't change the atomic number (the number of protons), so the atom is still a hydrogen atom. But they change its weight, so an atom with a proton and a neutron is called heavy hydrogen or, more commonly, deuterium. A hydrogen atom with two neutrons is called tritium.

Chemistry deals mostly with the effects of protons and electrons. The weight of an atom affects how it reacts with other atoms, but to a far smaller degree than its atomic number.

Atoms are extremely small. The nucleus of an atom is even smaller—so much so that an atom is mostly empty space. The electrons in the atoms are negatively charged, so they repel one another, and they also repel the electrons in other atoms. The reason you don't fall through your chair is that the electrons in your pants repel the electrons in the chair. But the atoms in your pants and the chair are still mostly empty space.

What chemicals do you find in everyday life?

Everything is a chemical. All of what we call things are made of atoms. A chemical is just something made of atoms.

But to stop there would be to ignore the common use of the term *chemical*, which is used to mean something made by chemists, as opposed to something found in nature. So while water is a chemical and vodka is a mixture of chemicals, neither is considered a "chemical" by people who lack an understanding of chemistry. Rubbing alcohol, a mixture very much like vodka but even more poisonous, is generally considered to be a chemical by such people, even if the distinctions are hard to understand.

So gasoline may or may not be considered a chemical by people who don't understand chemistry. But the additives that are in the gasoline to make it work better are all considered chemicals.

To many people, chemicals are anything listed in an ingredients label that they don't understand or that smells unusual. The acid that they put into their swimming pools is a chemical, but the same acid they produce in their stomachs to digest food is not.

So the things in everyday life that are considered chemicals are generally those substances used to clean, to disinfect, to prevent spoilage, to color, to glue, or to medicate.

Sometimes whether something is called a chemical depends on how it is used. If ethanol is in paint thinner, it is a chemical. If the same ethanol is in vodka, it is not a chemical. If sodium chloride is in your shampoo, it is a chemical. On your potato chips, it is not.

What does the periodic table of elements have to do with chemistry?

Elements are the smallest, simplest things a chemist works with. Everything else is built from elements.

Physics deals with things smaller than atoms. Chemistry deals with atoms. Even when chemists talk about smaller things, like protons and electrons, it is how they affect atoms or interact with atoms that the chemist is concerned about. The periodic table of the elements is in one sense just a list of all the building blocks that chemists play with. It starts with the smallest atom, hydrogen, and goes on up, adding one proton at a time to get through all of the known elements.

But the table is also *periodic*. It reflects the fact that as protons are added, their corresponding electrons can only be added into defined energy levels. Most of chemistry deals with the outermost electrons, since those are the ones that interact with other atoms. And every time an energy level is filled, the next electron added becomes a single outer electron, in a higher energy level. That makes the element behave like the one above it in the periodic table, because all of the elements in a column have the same number of electrons in their outermost shell.

This periodicity allows us to predict the behavior of elements scientists have yet to discover. Before the elements scandium, gallium, technetium, and germanium were discovered, their properties were predicted because there were "holes" in the periodic table where an element should have been. Likewise, the element protactinium was predicted before it was discovered. The same goes for the element hafnium.

How do elements get their names?

Some elements were named in ancient times, and we don't know the exact origins. Gold, silver, copper, lead, tin, iron, zinc, and carbon were all known to the ancients, and their names come from attributes such as their color, where they were originally found, or what their uses were. The word *carbon* comes from the Latin word for "coal" and *gold* comes from the Latin word for "yellow."

Other elements were discovered by chemists, who gave them names that we have some history for. *Hydrogen* means "water maker" because when it burns, we get water. It was discovered by Henry Cavendish but named by Antoine Lavoisier in 1783. Helium was first discovered by its spectral lines in the sun and was named after the Greek word for the sun.

Potassium was discovered in 1807 by Humphrey Davy and named after the material it was extracted from—potassium hydroxide, or potash, which was literally pot ash, the ashes that remain in a pot after burning vegetable matter.

Other elements were named after countries or continents: francium, polonium, europium, gallium, germanium, and americium. Some were named after people: rutherfordium, seaborgium, bohrium, meitnerium, roentgenium, copernicium, curium, fermium, einsteinium, mendelevium, nobelium, and lawrencium. Uranium, neptunium, and plutonium were named for planets. Palladium was named after an asteroid, which was named for a Greek goddess. Other gods gave thorium, selenium, and mercury their names, although the last may have been named for a planet that was named for a god.

Some elements are named for the towns, universities, or laboratories where they were discovered: berkelium, dubnium, hassium, darmstadtium, hafnium, terbium, ytterbium, erbium, yttrium, and californium.

How does gas cook our food and heat our homes?

By premixing the gas with air. When gas is allowed to escape into the air through a tube and then set alight, it burns with a yellow flame, called a *luminous flame*. It is luminous and yellow because it produces carbon soot that is heated until it glows yellow.

The presence of unburned carbon soot is an indication that the gas is not burning completely and some of the energy available in the gas is wasted. The gas is not mixing well with the air before it burns.

If some air is mixed with the gas before it reaches the flame, then more of the gas will be able to burn, and the result will be a hotter flame without any soot. Hotter flames burn blue instead of yellow and are not as bright, because there is no soot to heat to incandescence.

To mix air with the gas before it reaches the flame, a gas stove has a small opening for the gas, to make it jet out quickly into the air. It also has holes in the tube so the jet of unburned gas can draw in air through what is called the Venturi effect. The air and the gas mix thoroughly in the tube as the mixture travels to the openings in the burner. The openings are small holes, so that the flame does not travel back down into the tube. You can see the flames are blue and have little or no soot, and they start a little bit away from the holes in the burner.

Other gas heating devices work the same way. If you have a gas heater in your house, it premixes the air before igniting it. A gas clothes dryer also does this. In a chemist's laboratory, the Bunsen burner also has a small gas jet that sucks up air from holes in the tube and mixes the air and gas before burning it at the far end of the tube.

To get the hottest flames, a large amount of air is used, so that all of the gas burns. To allow this to happen without igniting the gas and air too early and in the wrong place, a screen of metal can be used to separate the flame from the gas and air mixture. The flame cannot get past the screen, since the metal draws off too much of the heat. A burner with this design is called a Meker burner, and this concept is also used in gas stoves for the kitchen, where the tiny exit holes act as the screen.

Why is lotion so oily?

and . . .

Why is oil so oily?

Oil lubricates things. A *lubricant* is a film of liquid that prevents parts from touching, so they slide easily past one another.

When you get a lubricant on your fingers, one finger can't feel the other—they only feel the lubricant. They slide past one another, and we say they feel oily, since most oils make good lubricants.

Lubricants generally work because their molecules bind more tightly to the parts that would otherwise rub together than they do to one another. The oil added to machines sticks to the metal parts, so it stays on the metal as a coating. But the coatings themselves do not stick to one another and instead just glide by.

Oil on your fingers works the same way to make your fingers slip past one another and thus feel slippery. Soap is also a good lubricant for fingers because one end binds to the skin and the other end is an oil, which does not bind to the oil ends of other soap molecules.

Many lotions contain oils. This is to prevent moisture loss from the skin, which a coating of oil will do. What people don't like is a greasy feeling. Grease is a thick oil or fat that is only a lubricant when under pressure. It is thicker and does not allow the skin surfaces to easily slide past one another.

Unsaturated oils can oxidize, which can make them form a plastic film that feels sticky and unclean. Lotions fight this in two ways: by adding ingredients that prevent oxidation, like vitamin E (tocopheryl acetate) and vitamin C (ascorbic acid, or ascorbyl palmitate), or by using saturated oils like mineral oil, which stays liquid and does not oxidize.

Most moisturizing lotions actually don't add much moisture to the skin. Instead, they use oils and fats to prevent moisture loss. After all, it is easy to moisturize your skin in a shower or a bath. The problem is keeping it moist after you leave the water.

Why does air leak out of a balloon?

Balloons are made of latex rubber. Latex rubber is a polymer—that is, a material made from long molecules that tangle up like spaghetti. And just like spaghetti, there are spaces in between the molecules that can let smaller molecules through.

The real question about balloons is why it takes so long for the air to leak out. In 1831, a man named Thomas Graham figured it out. It turns out that all gas molecules have the same average energy if they are at the same temperature. The energy of a gas molecule is a combination of how heavy it is and how fast it is moving. That means that if there are two molecules at the same temperature, but one is lighter than the other, the lighter one must be moving faster.

Fast-moving molecules leak faster than slow-moving ones.

The lightest gas molecule is hydrogen. It has an atomic weight of 2. The second lightest is helium, which has an atomic weight of 4. To find out how much faster hydrogen leaks from a balloon than helium, divide the square root of the heavier weight by the square root of the lighter one. So hydrogen leaks 1.414 times as fast as helium.

An oxygen molecule has an atomic weight of 32. It stays in the balloon four times as long as hydrogen. Air is mostly nitrogen molecules, with an atomic weight of 28. Nitrogen stays in the balloon 3.74 times as long as hydrogen.

One would expect butane, a gas whose molecules have four carbons and ten hydrogens, weighing 58, to stay in the balloon over five times longer than hydrogen, and 1.414 times longer than air (which has an average weight of about 29). But butane leaks out of the balloon surprisingly fast. I suspect that the butane is reacting with the latex rubber, either making it stretch out more, so it is thinner, or actually dissolving the rubber a little bit, so the long molecules are separated by butane molecules, which can then leak out quickly.

What makes an acid not good?

There are several ways to interpret the question, and so there are several answers. That makes it more fun.

It is not good to get acid in your eye. It hurts. The acid changes the shape of the proteins in your eye and skin, so those proteins don't work the way they normally do. Your body responds to this by sending pain signals to your brain, so you stop putting acid in your eye.

In your stomach, acid is produced by your body to help you digest your food and to kill microorganisms that might make you sick. It changes the protein called pepsin into the right shape to

PROJECT: BUTANE BALLOON

Materials

Butane lighter refill can (available at drug-
stores or hardware stores)
Freezer
Balloons (preferably large, 12-inch diameter)
Oven mitts
Kitchen scale (optional)

Adult supervision required

I love showing people how to do fascinating new things with ordinary objects and materials they might have around the house. This project plays with butane and has some very interesting results without ever even lighting it on fire. Butane is flammable, though, so throughout this experiment, make sure to **keep it away from open flames**.

You will need some time for preparation. An hour ought to do, but most of it will be just waiting. You also need a butane lighter refill can and some balloons. The large 12-inch-diameter balloons will work best.

First, put the can of butane into the freezer. Make sure the freezer is set to its coldest setting (this will also make your frozen food last longer). You want the butane to be as cold as the freezer compartment can make it.

Butane has a very interesting property. It is a liquid at $-0.5°$ Celsius ($31.1°$ Fahrenheit). Above this temperature, the liquid butane will boil, becoming a gas.

You may have seen transparent butane lighters, where you can easily see the level of butane liquid in them. Butane is a liquid at room temperature when it is under pressure. It does not take a lot of pressure to keep butane liquid. At 2.6 atmospheres of pressure, it will remain liquid up to 100° Fahrenheit (39° Celsius). This is why it can be stored as a liquid in little clear plastic lighters.

On a cold winter's day, when the temperature is a few degrees or more below freezing, a can of butane (or a butane lighter) won't work very well, since the contents will remain a liquid and won't have enough pressure to leave the container. Some camping stoves run on a mixture of butane and propane for this reason, since the propane will still be a gas in cold weather.

If the freezer has been set low enough, it will only take an hour or less for the butane can to get so cold that the butane will be a liquid.

Remove the butane can from the freezer using a towel or some oven mitts so your hands don't warm up the can. Stretch a balloon over the top of the can.

Turn the can upside down, pinch the plastic nozzle through the neck of the balloon, and push it toward the can. Liquid butane will pour into the balloon, along with some gaseous butane that has warmed up a bit. As the butane hits the balloon, some of it will boil into butane gas. The balloon will start to inflate a little.

Pinch the neck of the balloon and remove it from the can, and tie it closed.

The first thing to notice is that frost forms on the outside of the balloon where the liquid butane has made the rubber very cold.

Hold the balloon in your hand. The cold liquid butane will boil from the warmth of your hand. You can feel it boiling, even though it is below freezing in temperature. It makes a hissing sound, and the bubbles vibrate the balloon.

The balloon continues to get bigger. At some point, all of the liquid butane has turned into butane gas. As the gas warms to room temperature, the balloon will get a little bit bigger, but not as quickly as it did when the liquid was boiling.

The next thing to notice is that the balloon

feels heavy. This was not surprising when it had a puddle of liquid in it and it was small, but now it is a big balloon full of gas. Yet the weight has not changed perceptibly.

If you have a kitchen scale, you can investigate further. An empty balloon weighs about 3 grams.

A balloon full of air still weighs about 3 grams. But a balloon full of butane gas weighs 12 grams.

Butane is denser than air, so any volume of butane will weigh more than that volume of air. And since air is neutrally buoyant in the air around us, it does not register on the scale. But the butane sinks in air and presses down on the scale.

The third fascinating thing to do with the butane balloon is to hold it up to your ear. The dense gas in the roughly spherical balloon acts as a lens for sound waves. Turn your head (with the balloon still against your ear) until some source of sound, like a radio or a television or someone talking, has to go through the balloon to get to your ear.

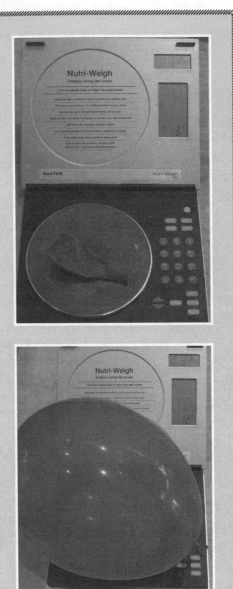

When the balloon is directly between your ear and the sound, the volume suddenly gets louder. The balloon lens is acting like a telescope for sound.

help break down the proteins in your food. Stomach acid also helps break the food down into smaller pieces, so it can be absorbed in your intestines.

The stomach makes the acid by separating neutral salts into an acid and a base. The acid is hydrochloric acid, and the base is bicarbonate. The bicarbonate stays in the stomach lining, to protect the cells there from the acid. The acid can then digest the food without digesting the stomach itself.

Sometimes the acid in your stomach gets into your esophagus, the tube leading into the stomach. If you have eaten too much and lie down, this is more likely to happen. The esophagus does not have the protective bicarbonate that the stomach lining has, so the acid hurts the delicate esophageal walls. This is called heartburn, or acid reflux. You have to sit up, or stand up, until your stomach empties enough to lie down and not spill acid into the esophagus.

Another way an acid can be "not good" is if it is no longer as acidic as it needs to be. The acid in batteries is needed for them to work properly. If it is diluted or neutralized, then the batteries won't work.

What is matter?

Matter is anything that has mass and takes up space. Mass is what gives things weight on Earth. If something feels heavy, it is matter. But the helium in a balloon is also matter. It only floats because the air around the balloon is heavier.

Most of the matter you encounter every day is made up of atoms. Your body, the ground under your feet, and the air you breathe are all made of atoms.

Inside the atoms, there are protons and neutrons in the nucleus and electrons in clouds around the nucleus. All of these particles have mass and take up space.

Protons and neutrons are in turn made up of even smaller particles, called quarks. And there is a whole zoo of particles that are seen when atoms smash together, with names like muons, taus, and neutrinos.

There are also things that aren't matter. These are called particles, but they have no mass and they take up no space. They carry force, and matter reacts to these forces. The photon carries the electromagnetic force and allows us to see, to feel heat, to send radio signals, and to take X-ray pictures. Other force-carrying particles are bosons and gluons.

Scientists also suspect that there is a lot of matter in the universe that we cannot see. We call it *dark matter*, and it is responsible for keeping galaxies from flying apart. It may be made up of particles that we have not yet detected. Some of it is undoubtedly neutrinos and black holes, but there seems to be far too much of it to be made up of just those things we know about.

What do gluons have to do with chemistry?

Nothing. Chemistry is the study of how atoms combine with other atoms. Gluons are force-carrying particles that hold quarks together to form protons and neutrons in atomic nuclei.

While we would not have atoms without gluons, gluons do not participate in the reactions that join atoms together to form molecules. What holds atoms together is the electromagnetic force, in the form of positive charges in the nucleus and negatively charged electrons.

Electrons move easily from one atom to another. Protons (hydrogen nuclei) are easily exchanged in reactions between acids and bases. But gluons stay inside the nucleus and don't play any part in sticking one atom to another.

What is hydrogen sulfate?

There are two hydrogen sulfates.

There is the hydrogen sulfate ion (also called the bisulfate ion), which has a sulfur atom, four oxygen atoms, and a hydrogen atom.

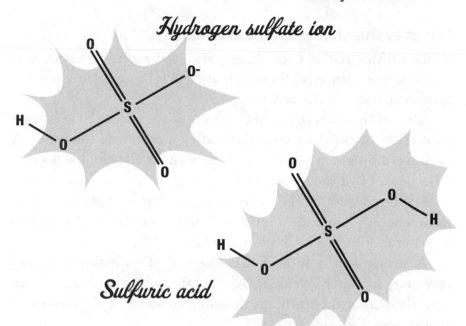

Hydrogen sulfate ion

Sulfuric acid

It has an extra electron (which makes it an ion) that hangs around one of the oxygen atoms.

If that lone extra electron attracts a proton (making a hydrogen atom) you get the other hydrogen sulfate. Because it has two hydrogens, it would be dihydrogen sulfate.

A more common name for this molecule is sulfuric acid. This is a powerful acid that is widely used in industry. It is the acid used in lead-acid car batteries.

A similar sounding molecule is hydrogen sulfide.

Hydrogen sulfide is a poisonous gas and is familiar as the smell of rotten eggs.

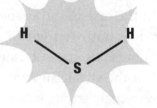

Hydrogen sulfide

What is the strongest kind of acid?

While sulfuric acid is a very strong acid, there are some acids that are even more powerful. In fact, if an acid is more acidic than sulfuric acid, it is called a *superacid*.

Most of the acids you might encounter are molecules that react with water by breaking up and donating a proton to the water. A proton is a hydrogen nucleus, and the water molecule that accepts it becomes a hydronium ion, H_3O^+.

Hydrogen chloride (HCl), for example, breaks apart in water to form a negative chloride ion Cl^- and donates its hydrogen nucleus to water to form the hydronium ion H_3O^+.

A strong acid is an acid that loses all of its hydrogen nuclei (protons) in water. Weak acids, like the acetic acid in vinegar, don't lose all of their protons in water, so some of the molecules stay intact.

The carborane superacid $H(CHB_{11}Cl_{11})$ is a million times stronger than sulfuric acid. It donates a proton very easily.

But while the ease with which an acid donates a proton is how the strength of an acid is defined, that is not what makes the acid corrosive, which may have been the main point of the question. What makes an acid corrosive is what is left behind after the proton leaves.

In the case of hydrofluoric acid, HF, what is left is the very reactive fluoride ion, and hydrofluoric acid reacts with almost anything. It even reacts with glass, so it can't be stored in glass bottles.

In the case of carborane, what is left behind is a very stable ion that does not react with much. So although it is the strongest of the superacids, it can be stored in a glass jar.

But the strong superacid fluoroantimonic acid ($HsbF_6$) is both an extremely strong superacid and quite corrosive.

Another famously corrosive acid is a mixture of one part nitric acid to three parts hydrochloric acid. It is called *aqua regia* ("royal water"), because it can dissolve the noble metals gold and platinum.

What does hydrogen chloride do?

Hydrogen chloride (HCl) is a gas. It is made up of two atoms, hydrogen and chlorine. It dissolves very easily in water, where it breaks down into a positively charged hydrogen nucleus (a proton) and a negatively charged chlorine ion. The proton immediately reacts with a water molecule to form the hydronium ion H_3O^+.

The result of dissolving the gas in water is called hydrochloric acid. It is a very useful acid—it cleans tarnish and rust off metals, it etches concrete, and it is used in swimming pools to neutralize the water (which is often slightly basic due to other chemicals in the water).

But hydrogen chloride gas is also interesting by itself. It will react with ammonia vapors in the air to form ammonium chloride, which is a solid. A fun thing to do (*with adult supervision*) is to put a little diluted hydrochloric acid on one paper towel and some ammonium hydroxide solution on another paper towel and bring them together. The vapors combine in the air, and the solid ammonium chloride particles look like smoke. (See the "Smoking Hands" project on page 4 for another version of this trick, and some *important safety guidelines*.)

The chlorine atom in hydrogen chloride holds on to electrons very tightly. The electron that would normally be associated with the hydrogen is strongly attracted to the chlorine and ends up spending most of its time on that side of the molecule.

This behavior leaves one side of the molecule positive and the other side negative, forming what is called a polar molecule. Water is also a polar molecule, and polar molecules attract one another because of their electrical charges. Hydrogen chloride gas combines with water vapor in the air to form hydrochloric acid vapor.

Why does snow melt?

It's a matter of balance. In chemistry, the word for balance is *equilibrium*. If something is in equilibrium, the amounts of things in it stay unchanged.

A snowflake is in equilibrium between solid water and liquid water. The bulk of the snowflake is solid, but at the surface there is a layer of liquid water, and some of that surface water escapes to become the gas water vapor. Molecules of water can also escape directly from the solid ice into the air to become water vapor without becoming a liquid first.

What keeps the snowflake intact is equilibrium. For each water molecule that leaves the ice to become water or water vapor, there is a molecule of water or water vapor that crystallizes onto the surface of the ice.

If the balance is disturbed, more atoms will solidify, forming more ice, or more atoms will liquefy, forming more water. The balance (or shift in the equilibrium) can be changed by changing the temperature or changing the pressure.

Heat is the motion of molecules. If heat is added to something, it raises the temperature, which is the speed of the molecules. In ice, the molecules are bouncing around against one another, vibrating back and forth. If the speed at which they bounce is increased, they can jostle loose and become liquid water.

If the pressure is increased, the water molecules on the outside of the ice are pushed back toward the ice, where they have a better chance of sticking to the other molecules there. So increasing the pressure makes more ice, and decreasing the pressure makes more water or water vapor.

Why do people put salt on icy roads?

Salt melts the ice. When you read about snow melting in the answer above, you saw that there is a balance between how many molecules froze onto the ice and how many molecules in the ice melted into the surrounding water. You saw that you could add heat or lower the pressure to tip the balance in favor of melting.

There is another way to tip the balance. Salt water doesn't freeze until it reaches almost −6° Fahrenheit (−21° Celsius). If salt is added to the water at the surface of the ice, the ice still melts at the same rate (that hasn't changed), but the water no longer freezes onto the ice until the temperature drops to −6° F.

It takes heat to melt ice. The ice can get that heat from the air or water around it, if that is warmer than the ice. The ice stays the same temperature (the freezing point), but the salt water around it gets colder as it loses heat melting the ice. Eventually the salt water reaches −6° F, and we are back in equilibrium again, with water freezing onto the ice as fast as it melts off it.

So if the temperature outside is below −6° F, salt won't melt the ice. You have to use something that freezes at an even lower temperature. A calcium chloride solution freezes at −20° F (−29° C), so it is used instead of the cheaper salt when the temperature is really low.

Why does ice float?

and . . .

Does ice weigh more than water?

No. I'm assuming the question refers to equal volumes of each, so it is really asking which is denser, water or ice.

You can see that ice floats in water, so it must be less dense than the water. To understand why that might be, you need to look closely at a molecule of water.

A water molecule forms a lopsided tetrahedron. The two hydrogens are at two corners of the pyramid, and the other two corners have pair of electrons. The electrons repel one another, and that causes the tetrahedron to be somewhat lopsided, so the angle between the two hydrogens is 104.5° instead of the 109.5° that a perfect tetrahedron would have.

The hydrogens are slightly positive, and the electron pairs are slightly negative, so if it was cold enough the molecules would stick together with a hydrogen of one molecule attracting the electron pair of another. This arrangement makes a six-sided crystal, and the molecules are about 9 percent farther apart than they would be if they were just randomly jumbled together, as they are in liquid water.

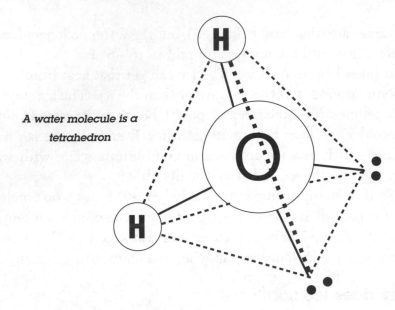

A water molecule is a tetrahedron

This is why an iceberg has 91 percent of its volume underwater and only 9 percent above the water. You can see this when you look at an ice cube floating in a glass of lemonade.

Water generally has air dissolved in it. As the water molecules form nice crystals of ice, the air comes out of solution. This forms tiny bubbles of air in the ice, which is why most ice cubes look white instead of clear. The bubbles make the ice float even higher than it would without them.

You can make ice without bubbles. Boil some water, so that most of the air leaves the water. Then transfer the water to the ice cube tray and freeze it. If there are still some bubbles in the ice, you can thaw the ice again, letting the bubbles escape, and refreeze it. The result will be crystal-clear ice cubes.

How is organic chemistry different from regular chemistry?

Organic chemistry is the study of carbon compounds. Carbon is special. It is small, having only six electrons. Two of them are in the low energy inner cloud, leaving four in the outer cloud where they can form bonds with other atoms. These two things are what make carbon special.

Being small, carbon can easily fit into molecules that would not have room for larger atoms. Being small also means that the electrons are close to the nucleus, so strong bonds can be formed.

Having four outer electrons means that carbon also has four empty slots for electrons from other atoms, since the second electron shell has room for eight electrons. Carbon can form lots of bonds with other atoms, forming long chains, loops, sheets, branching tree-like structures, and many other forms. This versatility is what leads to life. We call carbon chemistry *organic* because life is based on carbon compounds.

Organic chemistry is the study of carbon compounds whether or not they come from living things. We see carbon compounds in interstellar dust, inside meteorites, in coal and petroleum, and in the flames as carbon-based fuels burn. Organic chemistry is usually thought of as the chemistry of compounds that have a C-H bond (carbon bonded to hydrogen), although there are organic molecules that have no hydrogen, such as Teflon.

The study of chemical reactions in living things is a separate branch of chemistry called *biochemistry*. Of course, the two fields (organic chemistry and biochemistry) are closely related and overlap in many areas. Inorganic chemistry also overlaps with organic chemistry, as many simple carbon compounds such as chalk and carbon dioxide are considered inorganic, even though both are usually made by living things.

What is biochemistry?

and . . .

How is biochemistry related to regular chemistry?

Living organisms have a very complex chemistry, producing proteins, carbohydrates, nucleic acids (including DNA and RNA), lipids (fats and oils), and other biomolecules such as hormones.

The study of these molecules, and especially of the processes involved in making these molecules, is called biochemistry. A closely related and overlapping field is called molecular biology. Genetics, which once dealt only with inheritance, is now mostly a branch of biochemistry or molecular biology, since the discovery of DNA and the ability to sequence an organism's genetic code.

Biochemistry links the functions of an organism to the proteins and other biomolecules involved in its makeup. Molecular biology relates the genes in an organism to the proteins and biomolecules that the genes code for. Genetics relates the genes of an organism to the functions of the organism. Together, the three disciplines form the foundation of modern biology and medicine.

There are groups of biomolecules that are of particular importance to biochemists. Four in particular are carbohydrates, lipids, proteins, and nucleic acids.

Carbohydrates are sugars and things made from sugar. They are called carbohydrates because they have a chemical formula in which there is one carbon for every water molecule. Simple sugars can be joined to form disaccharides (like table sugar) or longer chains of sugars like starch, cellulose, and pectin.

Lipids are long chains of carbons, attached at one end to a glycerin molecule by a fatty acid end. Short-chained lipids with kinked tails make oils. Longer chains, or chains that are flexible and unkinked, can lie flat against one another easily, forming more solid fats.

Proteins are long chains made up of molecules called amino acids. Your skin, hair, and muscles are made of protein, and proteins called enzymes control almost every chemical reaction that happens in your cells.

Nucleic acids are the building blocks of DNA and RNA, the long molecules that encode how proteins are made in cells. This is the code that determines whether an organism is a tree, a frog, or a human.

How many types of chemistry are there?

There are five main branches of chemistry, and then there are many subdivisions of chemistry that cover specialized fields.

The five main branches are inorganic chemistry, organic chemistry, analytical chemistry, physical chemistry, and biochemistry.

Biochemistry and organic chemistry have been discussed already. Inorganic chemistry is usually described as the chemistry organic chemistry does not deal with. Analytical chemistry is the study of the properties of matter and tools to discover those properties. Physical chemistry applies physics to the study of chemistry, including thermodynamics and quantum mechanics.

Sub-branches of chemistry include astrochemistry (the chemistry in stars and interstellar gas and dust), electrochemistry (what happens when electrical currents flow though chemicals), food chemistry, geochemistry (the study of the composition of the Earth), nuclear chemistry, polymer chemistry, spectroscopy, theoretical chemistry, and many more.

Why are there so many varieties in chemistry?

Because chemistry is too big a subject for any one person to fully understand, people specialize in one part of chemistry, usually the part that interests them the most. Someone who studies the chemistry of petroleum products might have little need to know about the chemistry that goes on in interstellar nebulae or the chemistry of snail mucus. A person studying DNA to find cures for cancer might not want to take time out to learn about how to make a better rubber band.

Specializing allows someone to concentrate on one area of chemistry and one set of chemical techniques that are important in that area. A molecular biologist has less need of a spectroscope than an astrochemist would, and an explosives chemist would have no use for a DNA sequencer.

Theoretical and quantum chemists might not need any equipment at all, other than paper, pencil, and perhaps (these days) a computer.

But industrial chemists might spend a lot of time designing chemical equipment to produce things more efficiently or more safely.

What are chemical bonds?

Chemical bonds are what hold things together. Electrons are attracted to protons. Protons are contained in the nucleus of the atom, and electrons crowd in as close as they can to the nucleus, attracted by the protons. But electrons repel one another, and only a few can occupy each energy level around the nucleus.

Electrons try to get as close as possible to a nucleus but are prevented from getting too close if the spots near the nucleus are already filled with other electrons. This means that if we have two atoms, and one has an electron far away from the nucleus and the other has an empty spot near the nucleus, the electron from the first atom can fall into the empty slot of the second atom.

Sometimes the electron actually leaves the first atom and joins the second. That leaves two ions. The first is positively charged, since it has one more proton than electron. The second is negatively charged, since it has an extra electron. These two ions are attracted to one another, because they have opposite charges.

In other cases, the electron doesn't fully leave the first atom. It falls into the empty slot in the second atom, but it still fills the outer slot in the first atom. The two atoms are held together by the attractions of their nuclei to the shared electron.

In the metallic elements, the outer electrons are very mobile, since they are far away from the nucleus and are attracted to all of the nearby nuclei by about the same amount. They move from nucleus to nucleus, always staying far out where the forces of attraction are fairly weak. The effect is that the positive nuclei are surrounded by a sea of negative electrons, flitting around from atom to atom.

How many types of bonds are in chemistry?

The first type of bond discussed in the previous answer, where the electron leaves the first atom and joins the second, is called an *ionic bond*. This kind of bond is found in molecules like sodium chloride (salt), where an atom that easily loses its outer electron (such as sodium) combines with an atom that has an empty slot very close to the nucleus (like chlorine) that is very good at attracting electrons.

The second type discussed, in which two nuclei share an electron, is called a *covalent bond*. These are very strong bonds, and they hold molecules together very well. Bonds between carbon atoms, or between carbon and hydrogen, are usually covalent bonds.

The third type of bond discussed is called a *metallic bond*, because it is characteristic of the bonds seen in metals.

All three of these bond types are bonds in which one or more electrons is involved. There are other kinds of bonds, usually much weaker than the first three, which form when, on average, less than a whole electron is involved.

We looked earlier at the *hydrogen bond* (in the discussion of water and chemistry, page 153) which forms between molecules rather than between individual atoms. Molecules are required because this kind of bond only happens when an electron spends more of its time around one atom in the molecule than around another atom. This makes one side of the molecule a little more negative and the other side a little more positive. The positive end of one molecule is then attracted to the negative end of another to make the hydrogen bond.

A similar set of effects, collectively called van der Waals forces (named after the Dutch scientist Johannes Diderik van der Waals) can happen even to single atoms. The electrons around two atoms can become correlated, so that when an electron in the first atom is on one side, so is an electron on the other atom, and when the electrons spin around the atom, they do so in synchrony, so that there is always a positive side of one atom facing the negative side of the other, creating an attraction.

How long has chemistry been around?

About 379,000 years after the universe began in the Big Bang, it had cooled enough for electrons to slow down enough to stick around protons, and the first atoms of hydrogen formed. Since scientists only know when the universe began to within 110 million years, they can't say exactly when this happened, except to say it was between 13.64 and 13.86 billion years ago.

People first started using techniques of chemistry sometime around 3,000 years ago, when they began extracting metals from ores, making beer and wine, and making pottery and glazes. The first controlled chemical reaction may have been fire.

Early attempts at understanding chemical reactions were largely unsuccessful, although the practice, called *alchemy*, led to many discoveries, including the production of several important acids, the practice of distillation, and other techniques still in use.

The beginnings of modern chemistry are usually traced back to 1661, with the publication of *The Sceptical Chymist* by Robert Boyle. Later, when Antoine Lavoisier developed the law of the conservation of mass, chemistry became a science, in which careful measurements allowed mathematical interpretation of the results of experiments.

One of the earliest people to systematize the investigation of chemical reactions was the Persian scientist Abu Musa Jābir ibn Hayyān, known as Geber to Europeans. Born in 721, Geber is credited with the invention of distillation. Much of his writings were deliberately hard to decipher, so that only other alchemists could read it, and this may be the origin of the word *gibberish*, from the name Geber. His main contribution was his stressing of the importance of experimentation in chemistry.

Can you change lead into gold?

I have never done this. But it can be done.

Although transforming base metals like lead into precious metals, specifically gold, was a goal of early alchemists, it is not actually chemistry. Chemistry deals with combinations of atoms, not with changing one element into another.

Transmuting elements is part of a branch of physics that deals with elemental particles. *Transmutation* (converting one element, such as mercury, into another, such as gold) occurs naturally. All of the elements heavier than lithium were created in stars by transmutation.

Nitrogen in the upper atmosphere is transmuted into radioactive carbon-14 by neutrons created when cosmic rays strike the upper atmosphere. The carbon-14 later decays back into nitrogen.

Scientists first realized that transmutation was taking place in 1901, when Ernest Rutherford and Frederick Soddy found that thorium was decaying into radium. Later, in 1917, Rutherford was able to transmute nitrogen into oxygen by bombarding it with helium nuclei (called *alpha particles*).

Making gold from other metals would be more expensive than buying gold that was mined from the ground. But when absolutely pure gold is needed, it may be cheaper to create gold from mercury (by bombarding it with gamma rays) than to try to extract the copper and silver impurities often found in natural gold.

Going in the other direction, making pure mercury from gold, is also useful, as the pure mercury can be used to make a kind of light source that is very pure.

What is the difference between radiation and radioactivity?

Radiation is anything that "radiates" away from something. In chemistry and physics, it refers to light, radio waves, X-rays, and gamma rays, as well as to particles such as neutrons, protons, helium nuclei (alpha particles), and electrons (beta particles).

Most forms of radiation humans encounter are harmless or even necessary for life. Without light and heat, there would be no life. We use radio waves for communication, and they pass through us without harm.

In medicine, radiation usually refers to *ionizing radiation*. This is radiation that has enough energy to strip electrons away from atoms, forming ions. Since electrons are what form the bonds between molecules in our bodies, ionizing radiation can change those bonds in harmful ways, creating burns or damaging DNA, which can cause cancer.

Radioactivity refers to something that happens to atoms that have too many or too few neutrons in them in proportion to the number of protons. These atoms are unstable and decay into more stable atoms by emitting radiation.

You read in the last question how radioactive carbon-14 decayed into nitrogen; it does so by changing a neutron into a proton and an electron (the latter of which speeds away as a beta particle). More famously, uranium goes through a series of radioactive decays into various elements, eventually turning into lead.

Radioactive elements produce many types of radiation as they decay. They can emit electrons, alpha particles, neutrons, neutrinos, and gamma rays (a form of high-energy X-rays). They can also produce larger atomic nuclei that fly away as the atom splits.

How do they make petroleum into jelly?

Actually, chemists extract the jelly from petroleum. Petroleum jelly is a mixture of hydrocarbon chains with lengths of 25 or more carbons. A hydrocarbon is just what it sounds like, a chain of carbons on which every carbon has hydrogens bound to it.

The length of the chains determines whether the hydrocarbon will be a liquid, like gasoline (with lengths from 6 to 10 carbons) or mineral oil, or a solid, like paraffin wax (with 20 to 40 carbons in the chain). Petroleum jelly is in between, with around 25 carbons (there are a number of different molecules of different lengths in the mixture).

A crude black form of petroleum jelly was originally discovered by workers on oil rigs, as a gunk that fouled up the machinery. A chemist named Robert Chesebrough refined this into a white paste that has no color, odor, or taste and marketed it as Vaseline in 1872.

As a grease that prevents skin from drying out and keeps bacteria away from burns and wounds, Vaseline found many uses in the home medicine cabinet. It melts at a temperature close to human body temperature, so it becomes a near-liquid when applied to the skin.

You may know Chesebrough's name through the brand Chesebrough-Ponds, now a subsidiary of Unilever. The brand includes Ponds Cold Cream and Cutex nail polish remover.

Why do chemicals foam up?

Chemicals foam up because they release gas. The most familiar foaming reaction is probably that of baking soda and vinegar. A similar reaction is what makes pancake batter rise. Sodium bicarbonate is a salt of a strong base (sodium hydroxide) and a weak acid (carbonic acid). When you add an acid to a salt of another acid, you generally release a gas that makes the second acid when mixed with water. Baking soda releases carbon dioxide gas, which makes carbonic acid when mixed with water. You have swallowed carbonic acid—it is the bubbly water to which sugar and flavorings are added to make flavored sodas.

Another familiar reaction that produces bubbles of gas is that of hydrogen peroxide when it meets a catalyst that breaks it down into water and oxygen. That catalyst is a protein called *catalase* that most living things produce, because hydrogen peroxide is a harmful byproduct of metabolism, and the catalase breaks it down.

Reacting any of several metals (such as aluminum, magnesium, or zinc) with an acid will release hydrogen gas. The metal replaces the hydrogen in the acid, leaving a salt (such as aluminum chloride if the acid was hydrochloric acid) and bubbles of hydrogen.

Electricity can create bubbles of gas. In water, electricity will release hydrogen bubbles from one electrode and oxygen from the other. In salt water, chlorine gas is released instead of oxygen.

To make bubbles into a foam, it helps to have some molecules that reduce the surface tension of in the liquid the bubbles are in. Soap and detergents will do this. By lowering the surface tension, the soap stabilizes the thin layer of water around the bubble in the foam. Something called the *Marangoni effect* says that water will flow into the area that has the lowest surface tension. As the bubble stretches, the concentration of soap is reduced. This causes water to rush in to strengthen the thinnest layers in the bubble.

What is hydrogen peroxide?

Hydrogen peroxide is two atoms of oxygen, each attached to a hydrogen atom. You can think of it as a water molecule with an extra oxygen in the middle.

The oxygen we breathe has two oxygen atoms in it—we call it molecular oxygen. In molecular oxygen, the two atoms share two electrons, in what we call a double bond.

When two oxygens are connected with a single bond, we call it a peroxide. Hydrogen peroxide is the simplest example of a peroxide molecule.

Pure hydrogen peroxide is a liquid a little heavier and thicker (more viscous) than water. It is a strong oxidizer and can start fires if it contacts flammable materials like wood or paper.

In the home, dilute solutions of hydrogen peroxide are used to disinfect and bleach. Three percent hydrogen peroxide is used to

Hydrogen peroxide   *Molecular oxygen*

clean wounds and as a mouth rinse to kill bacteria. Stronger solutions are used to bleach hair.

Cells produce hydrogen peroxide as a byproduct of metabolism. But hydrogen peroxide is also used by the immune system as a signal that attracts white blood cells to an infection.

A 3 percent solution of hydrogen peroxide will produce ten times its volume in oxygen if a catalyst (such as blood or dry yeast) is added. Most common metals will also act as a catalyst for the dissociation of hydrogen peroxide into oxygen and water. Adding a catalyst to hydrogen peroxide is thus an easy way to generate oxygen.

What is a soda can made out of?

These days, soda cans are usually made of an *alloy*, or metallic mixture, consisting mostly of aluminum with about 1 percent manganese and 1 percent magnesium. The extra metals give the aluminum more strength and make it easier to form. Other metals are in the alloy in much smaller quantities, including copper, gallium, iron, silicon, titanium, vanadium, and zinc. Some of these are added deliberately to improve the alloy, while others are present only because they would be difficult to remove from the raw materials used to make the alloy.

The lid of a soda can is made from a different alloy, which contains up to 5 percent magnesium. This alloy is more expensive and not as strong as the alloy used for the body of the can, but it is more easily formed into the complex easy-open top. This is why the top of the can is so much smaller in diameter than the rest of the can—it makes it cheaper, and a smaller lid is stronger, so the weaker, more expensive alloy is not a problem. The bottom of the can is also made smaller in diameter so that the cans will stack.

Soda cans are lacquered with plastic, both to prevent the acids in the contents from attacking the aluminum and to keep the outside of the can from reacting with things it contacts in shipping and storage. Food-grade petroleum jelly and food grade waxes are used as lubricants when the cans are constructed and crimped closed.

Soda cans are designed to hold a maximum pressure of 95 pounds per square inch. This is much more than the contents of the can are usually under and provides some margin for heat and shock in shipping.

What is the difference between Fahrenheit and Celsius?

The two temperature scales were developed by two different people, and they use two different ideas of where to put the zero and 100 marks.

Daniel Fahrenheit based his original temperature scale on three temperatures. The coldest he had available—ice in a brine made from salt and ammonium chloride—would be the zero point (0°). He wanted human body temperature to be near 100°. His third temperature was the melting point of ice. To make it easier to mark his thermometers, he made the freezing point 32° and the human temperature 96°, so he could make the markings by simply cutting the interval between 96° and 32° in half six times.

Later, the scale was adjusted so that water boiled at 212° and froze at 32°. This made human body temperature closer to 98°. The interval between freezing and boiling was 180°, an easy number to divide into parts.

In 1744 a different scale was created, based on one made by Anders Celsius a couple years earlier. His scale used the freezing point of water as 100° and the boiling point of water at sea level as 0°. After his death, the scale was reversed so that higher temperatures had higher numbers.

Because a degree was $\frac{1}{100}$ of the difference between melting and boiling, it was called the *centigrade scale* for over 200 years. But that term was also used for other measurements, and the international standards bureau changed the name to Celsius in 1948.

What makes bridges so strong?

Concrete, steel, and geometry. There are many kinds of bridges, and as many ways for them to be strong.

Suspension bridges, such as the Golden Gate Bridge in San Francisco, get their strength from steel and geometry. The bridge is mostly in tension: the forces on it try to pull it apart more than they try to compress it. Steel has very high strength under tension, so steel cables are used to build the bridge. The towers supporting the bridge are under compression and are made of steel, sitting on enormous concrete piers.

Other bridges are often made using arches of concrete. Concrete has very high compression strength, and an arch is almost entirely under compression instead of tension. This is due to the geometry of the arch, which channels the load downward into the ground.

Most smaller bridges, such as those used for freeway overpasses, use a trick that combines the tensile strength of steel with the compression strength of concrete. Reinforced and pre-stressed concrete are building techniques where steel reinforcements are added to concrete where it will be under tension. Little or no reinforcing is needed where the structure is only under compression forces. In a bridge span, the steel will be on the bottom and the concrete on the top. As the bridge is loaded, the concrete compresses, and the steel pulls.

Pre-stressed concrete takes this one step further by putting the steel parts under tension before the concrete is poured.

Why do some things dissolve in water and others don't?

Water is a polar molecule, with one end positively charged and the other negatively charged. These charges interact with ionic bonds in substances like table salt. The water molecules surround the charged particles in the salt with oppositely charged ends of the water molecules. This reduces the effective charges on the sodium and chlorine ions, so they no longer attract one another as much as they did before.

The rest of the work of dissolving the salt is done by heat and by the motion of the water, both of which jostle the ions apart, so they can be surrounded by water molecules and isolated.

The polar nature of water is also why nonpolar molecules do not dissolve in water. Substances like oils, fats, and waxes have no charged parts to attract water molecules. The water molecules are attracted to one another by their charges, and they leave the nonpolar molecules alone. This pulling together of all the water molecules acts to pull them away from uncharged molecules, so oil and water don't mix.

Since water is denser than most oils, fats, and waxes, it falls to the bottom of the container, and the oil is left behind, on top.

Other materials, like metals, sand, rocks, or plastic, are also unaffected by water, and for the same reasons, only in reverse. The molecules in rocks and metals attract one another much more than they do water. So the metal atoms stick together and leave the water behind. Since they are generally heavier, they sink to the bottom, leaving the water on top.

What is plastic made of?

Plastic is long chains of small molecules called *monomers* that are joined together. The long chains are called *polymers*.

Your hair, your fingernails, and the tendons in your arms and legs are made of polymers. In those polymers (called *proteins*) the building blocks are called *amino acids*. They are chained together to form strong ropes of material to be used where strength is important.

You can make your own protein plastic from milk. Add some vinegar to nonfat milk, and it will curdle into white clumps of casein protein. You can compress this into a mold and let it dry into a hard plastic. Umbrella handles used to be made this way.

PROJECT:

EXTRACTING IODINE

Materials

Test tube with stopper or similar glass
    container, such as a small glass jar
    with lid
Tincture of iodine (available at drug-
    stores and pharmacies)
Water
Toluene solvent (available at hardware stores) or naphtha cigarette
    lighter fluid (available at drugstores)
Eyedropper or pipette
Glass jar with lid
Hair dryer with no-heat setting

Adult supervision required

One of the projects coming later uses crystals of the element iodine.

For someone like me, finding iodine crystals is as simple as reaching up to the top shelf in the lab. But for most of the readers of this book, the pure element is not so easy to come by.

However, there is a tiny bit of iodine in that bottle of tincture of iodine you can find at the pharmacy. There is about half a gram in each fluid ounce of the disinfectant.

Extracting the pure element is simple and demonstrates how clever chemists can be using simple supplies and materials. The principle is called *partitioning*, or sometimes *liquid-liquid extraction*. It takes advantage of the fact that some things dissolve more easily in one liquid than another.

The liquid in tincture of iodine is alcohol. Iodine does not dissolve well in alcohol, and dissolves even less well in water.

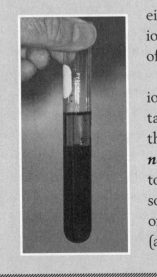

To get the elemental iodine to dissolve in either of these solvents, a little potassium iodide is added. The iodide ion helps more of the pure iodine dissolve.

Pour a small amount of the tincture of iodine into a test tube or a similar glass container with a stopper or lid, so it's no more than about one-sixth of the way full. (**Do not use a plastic container**, because the toluene we'll be adding in the next step dissolves plastic.) Then add an equal amount of water and an equal amount of toluene (available in stores either as a pure solvent or as naphtha cigarette lighter fluid). The water dilutes the alcohol and makes the iodine less soluble in the mixture. The toluene will float to the top, since it does not mix well with either alcohol or water.

Iodine dissolves easily in toluene. In the photo on the previous page you can see the bottom layer of 50 percent water and 50 percent tincture of iodine, and above it the layer of toluene, which has already started to get pinkish-violet from the iodine it has absorbed.

The next step is to stopper the test tube (or close the glass jar, etc.) and shake well for 15 to 20 seconds. The two layers will mix, and there will be some froth at the top, but when you stop shaking, the two layers will fairly quickly separate again. After 30 seconds of sitting still, the top layer of toluene can be seen stained a dark purple by the iodine it has extracted from the tincture, as in the photo above.

The next step is to use an eyedropper or a pipette to carefully remove as much of the top layer of dark purple toluene as you can into a glass jar, without getting any of the alcohol and water mixture in with it. There will be a little toluene left in the test tube, but that is OK.

Now you have a jar with dark purple toluene in it. You need

to evaporate the toluene while losing as little of the iodine as possible. Iodine slowly vaporizes at room temperature, but if you give the toluene a lot of flowing air, it will evaporate faster  than the iodine does. I used a blow dryer that had a setting that allowed the air to flow without any heat (heat would evaporate the iodine quickly). In a few minutes, the toluene had evaporated, and I had pure iodine crystals in the bottom of the jar.

Save the crystals by tightly closing the jar. You will need them for a later project, "Latent Fingerprints" (page 202).

Plastic plumbing pipes are made from monomers of vinyl chloride, joined together to make polyvinyl chloride plastic.

The carbon atoms join together into long chains in which every second carbon has a hydrogen and a chlorine atom instead of two hydrogens.

Another common plastic monomer is vinyl acetate.

Polyvinyl acetate, made from this monomer, is familiar as white school glue. It forms a flexible, translucent plastic that can be heated to change its shape.

CI

Vinyl chloride monomer

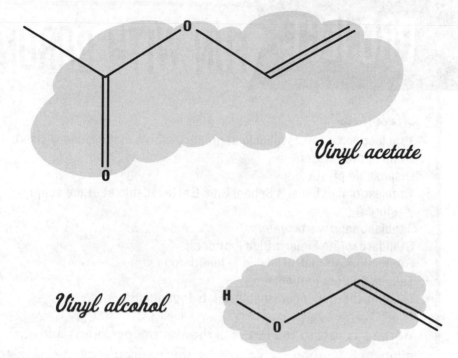

Vinyl acetate

Vinyl alcohol

Between 100 and 5,000 vinyl acetate molecules join up to form the long chains in the polymer.

A related polymer is polyvinyl alcohol. It is made of monomers of vinyl alcohol. This plastic is often combined with other monomers to make what are called *copolymers*. Changing the type of copolymer or the proportion of the two monomers can change the nature and properties of the plastic produced.

PROJECT: FUN WITH BORON

Materials

1 tablespoon borax (available at grocery stores in the laundry aisle)
1 cup hot tap water
Disposable plastic cup
1 tablespoon of Elmer's School Glue Gel (available at office supply stores)
3 tablespoons warm water
Standard white Elmer's Glue (optional)
Guar gum (optional, available at health food stores)
Talcum powder (optional)
Glow-in-the-dark or washable paints (optional)

Boron sits just to the left of carbon in the periodic table of the elements. Carbon, of course, is the molecule of life, able to make long strings of atoms called polymers. These make up things like DNA, protein, plastics, wood, and the fibers in our clothing. Boron is almost carbon. While it does not make long polymer strands by itself, it is quite useful for joining polymers together. When it does this, we call it *cross-linking*.

Cross-linking makes a polymer firmer. Depending on how much cross-linking happens, the result can be an oozy slime, a bouncing ball, or a firm, hard plastic.

In this project, you are going to start with a boron-containing molecule called borax. You may have some in your laundry room.

In water, borax dissolves to form the *borate anion*, a boron atom surrounded by OH (hydroxyl) groups.

Look at those four OH groups hanging on the boron. Those will be important in a minute.

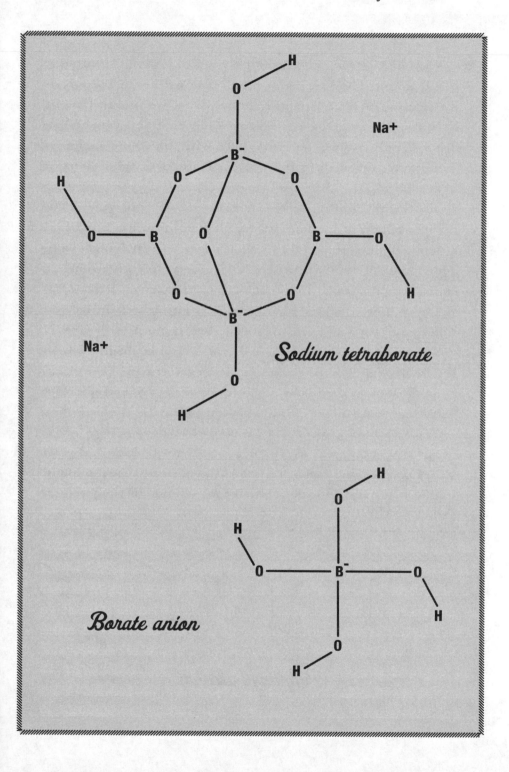

Sodium tetraborate

Borate anion

You have several choices of polymer to cross-link with our borate anion. The first one you will play with is called polyvinyl alcohol, or PVA for short. This is what we find in Elmer's School Glue Gel, the transparent blue glue you can find in office supply stores. You will play with the more common white glue, made from polyvinyl acetate (PVAc for short) a little later.

In the illustration below, notice that the polyvinyl alcohol (continued in the blue school glue gel) also has those OH groups dangling from every second carbon in the polymer chain. Those can interact with other OH groups to form what are called *hydrogen bonds*. In the OH group, the oxygen attracts the electrons more than the hydrogen does. This leaves the oxygen slightly negative and the hydrogen slightly positive. Two OH groups will thus be attracted to one another like magnets, with the positive end of one attracting the negative end of the other.

Now look at the illustration on the next page and see what happens when you add a borate anion to the PVA.

This form of cross-linking is easily broken, since hydrogen bonds are pretty weak as chemical bonds go. The result is not a strong plastic or a strong glue but a kind of slime that you might like to play with. But notice that two strands of the polymer

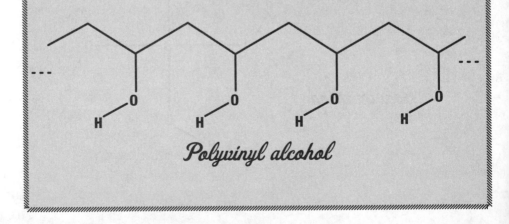

Polyvinyl alcohol

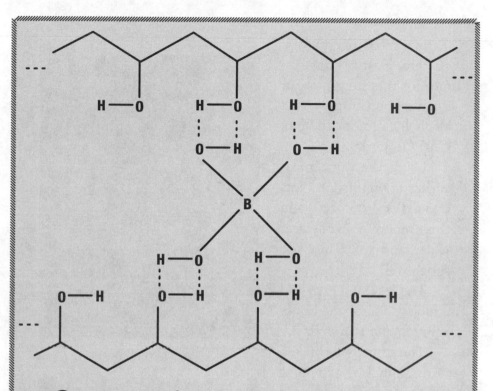

Borate cross-linked polyvinyl alcohol polymer

that used to be simply tangled up together like spaghetti are now joined by the borate, so you have something more like a net. A net is firmer than a tangle of strands.

To make slime, you will need a saturated solution of borax in water. That means you dissolve borax in hot water from the tap until no more will dissolve and then let it cool to room temperature. There will be some borax sediment at the bottom, and that tells you that it is a saturated solution. About a tablespoon of borax to a cup of water will do nicely. Feel free to use more borax; you can't screw it up by using too much.

In a separate cup (disposable plastic cups are nice for this step) pour in a tablespoon of polyvinyl alcohol (Elmer's School Glue Gel).

Using the same measuring spoon (so it gets cleaned a little bit) add three tablespoons of warm water, and stir. Rinse the spoon well after this.

The last step is to add a tablespoon of the borax solution and stir well.

The slime will thicken fairly quickly. Remove the thick mass and knead it in your hands for a while, stretching it and folding it. You can control how thick or runny it is by changing how much water there is in the mix.

Left to itself, the slime will melt into a puddle. But you can pick it up, roll it into a ball or a rope, and snap it into pieces. Then let it rest, and it oozes back into a puddle.

You can make another polymer toy very similar

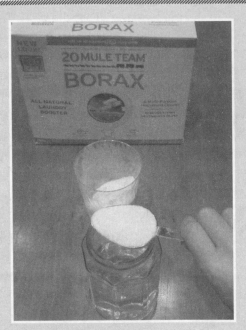

Making saturated borax solution

Measuring a tablespoon of polyvinyl alcohol

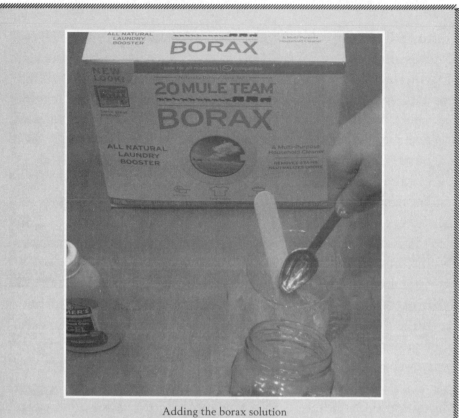

Adding the borax solution

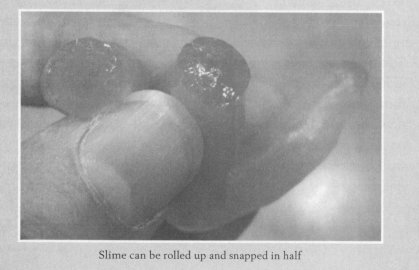

Slime can be rolled up and snapped in half

to Silly Putty by cross-linking poly-vinyl acetate (standard white Elmer's Glue) with borax. Five parts glue, four parts water, and one part saturated borax solution.

Like the original, it can be rolled into a bouncing ball, stretched slowly, or broken with a sharp pull, and it can transfer ink from newspapers.

Other polymers can also be cross-linked using borax. Try guar gum for making a nice slime. Additives can be added, such as talcum powder or glow-in-the-dark or washable paints, to change the texture and color.

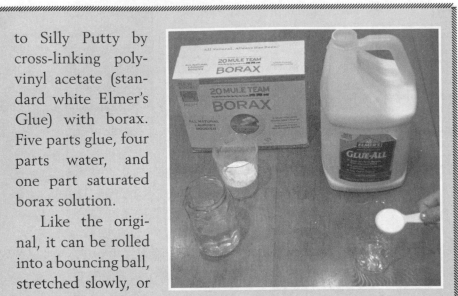

Making elastic putty

Transferring newsprint ink

9

Chemists

To someone fascinated with chemistry, the idea of being a chemist naturally comes to mind. But what does a chemist do all day? How is a chemist different from another kind of scientist? And how is chemistry used in other professions? Doctors, pharmacists, detectives, mechanics, janitors, farmers, firefighters—all kinds of people use chemistry every day, and they depend on their knowledge of chemistry to do their jobs and keep us safe, keep us fed, and keep things moving.

What are some things chemists do?

Some chemists study chemical reactions, such as the scientists who monitor both the ozone layer that protects us from the sun and the molecules that destroy ozone in the atmosphere. Other chemists create new kinds of molecules, either to cure diseases such as cancer or to make new plastics or new fibers for the latest fashions. There are millions of other examples, since chemistry is a very broad field.

Vicki Finkenstadt went to school on a basketball scholarship and became a chemist making plastics from corn starch. Mario Molina won a Nobel Prize in chemistry for his work on the decomposition of ozone. Dianne Gates studies how to clean up radioactive waste, such as that from the Fukushima nuclear power plant that was damaged by the 2011 tsunami in Japan. In studying how nuclear material is spread by weapons, she worked with explosives experts to set off a small bomb and examine the dispersal patterns of the debris.

Ean Warren works for the United States Geological Survey (USGS) in Menlo Park, California, where he studies the chemistry of ocean "dead zones" and how microbes once made a house explode. Lucy Yu is a food chemist who studies the natural antioxidants in whole wheat muffins and how to make healthier pizza crusts with more dietary fiber.

Joseph Francisco worked to discover how to make new superconducting materials before deciding to become a professor of chemistry. Haile Mehansho studies nutrition to find out how to eliminate problems that cause mental retardation and stunted growth. Katherine Glasgow researches plastics for new products. Bernard Gordon is president of his own chemical company, which designs water-degradable fishing line, reducing the environmental impact of sport fishing. Louis Rubens designs plastic foams and the reactions that create the gases in the foams.

How do people today use chemistry and science in their jobs?

Scientists are not the only people who use science to do what they do. And chemists are not the only ones who use chemistry.

Doctors need to know a lot of science to do their job, and they apply the scientific method to find out what is wrong and how best to fix it. Cooks who know a little chemistry can predict what will happen if they substitute ingredients in a recipe. Builders who pour concrete use chemistry every day. So do the people who adjust the chemicals in swimming pools to keep the water safe.

The scientific method can be applied to solve any problem, from determining what is wrong with a car when a mechanic is asked to fix it to finding out how best to improve education in schools. Knowing some science and how to interpret scientific results is important in selecting your congresspeople when you vote and in selecting the best people to see when you are ill.

Science keeps us safe. People who design cars and bridges use science to make sure they can handle the demands put on them. Doctors who work to prevent epidemics use science to predict where they will spread and how best to stop them. The people who make policy in government need to use science to prevent air and water pollution, to decide which energy sources to promote, and to provide the best foods and education to the people they represent.

How are chemists different from and similar to scientists?

Chemists are scientists. Chemistry is a branch of science, so anyone who practices chemistry is doing science.

The study of chemistry involves many parts of other sciences, so in some senses chemists also are sometimes physicists, physicians, biologists, sociologists, economists, mathematicians, astronomers, geneticists, or ecologists. For the same reasons, many scientists in fields other than chemistry end up doing a lot of chemistry. Medical scientists, geologists, botanists, meteorologists, volcanologists, mineralogists, and oceanographers all frequently use chemistry in what they do.

Science is a systematic approach to obtaining knowledge. It can be applied to anything. The scientific method has four parts:

- *Observing and measuring*
- *Forming a hypothesis*
- *Making a prediction*
- *Testing the hypothesis*

If you apply the scientific method to find out where you left your socks, you are doing science.

PROJECT: LATENT FINGERPRINTS

Materials

Glass microscope slide or other small glass object

Glass jar with cover (big enough to hold the microscope slide)

Paper towel

1 to 2 drops of superglue

Saucepan of water

Kitchen stove

Oven mitts

Jar of iodine crystals from "Extracting Iodine" project (page 187)

Business card, note card, or other small white card

Hairspray

Adult supervision required

When scientists provide help for law enforcement, that is called *forensic science*. In this project, you will act as crime lab chemists to develop latent fingerprints—that is, fingerprints that you normally cannot see and that can't be made visible by "dusting for prints."

You will use two different chemical techniques in this project. One is good for developing fingerprints on smooth surfaces such as glass or plastic. The other works for surfaces like paper.

The first technique uses superglue, known to chemists as *cyanoacrylate*. Superglue is a liquid that *polymerizes* (hardens) when it encounters water vapor. But a greasy fingerprint makes it harden faster, and that is the key to this technique.

Start out by making a nice fingerprint on a glass microscope slide (a conveniently small piece of glass—you can substitute a small jar or other glass object). Rub your finger on your nose or forehead where the oils from your skin are most pronounced, and carefully press your finger on the glass so as not to smudge the fingerprint.

Place the microscope slide in a glass jar. (I used a binder clip to make it stand up, but that is not really necessary.) Next, add a piece of paper towel, moistened with a bit of water. This will provide the water vapor for the glue to harden. Last, add a drop or two of superglue, being careful not to drop it on the slide or the paper but just on the bottom of the jar. You don't want to glue anything down accidentally.

Cover the jar tightly.

Now you want to boil the cyanoacrylate. It boils at a fairly low temperature compared to water, so the easy way to do this is to boil some water, then take the pan off the stove and put the jar into the almost-boiling water.

Look into the jar at where your fingerprint was on the glass slide. It will not take long before it starts to appear, as the cyanoacrylate vapor meets the greasy fingerprint and starts to

harden, leaving a white fingerprint visible on the glass.

If you leave it in the jar too long, the white ridges of the fingerprint will continue to grow more polymer until the ridges merge together and the fingerprint is ruined. So when it looks like a good sharp image of a fingerprint, open the jar and remove the glass slide. The print will look something like the picture below.

Since the superglue hardens into a white print, it would not help very much on a white piece of paper. Luckily, there is another technique for developing latent fingerprints that works very well on paper.

For this you will use the jar of iodine crystals we made in the project "Extracting Iodine" (page 187). By this time, there will probably not be any visible crystals in that jar, as they will have evaporated and then recondensed on the walls of the jar in a thin brown film. Don't worry, the iodine is still there and will work nicely for this project.

Rub your finger on your nose or forehead again and press it carefully but firmly on a white card, such as the

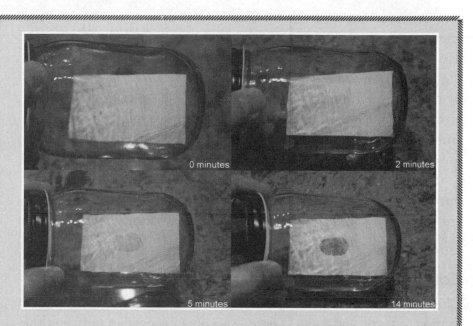

back of a business card or a 3-by-5 note card. If the card is too big to fit in the jar, cut it to size. Then simply drop it into the jar of iodine and close the lid again. In less than a minute, you will start to see a faint tan fingerprint appear. Wait a few more minutes, and the tan will develop into a nice dark brown that clearly shows the ridges of your fingerprint.

Make sure you close the jar of iodine so it doesn't evaporate away. You can use it again many times before you have to make a new batch of iodine.

The iodine print will gradually fade away if left in the open air. To preserve it, you can spray it with a little hairspray. The hairspray leaves a thin coating of plastic that holds the iodine in place.

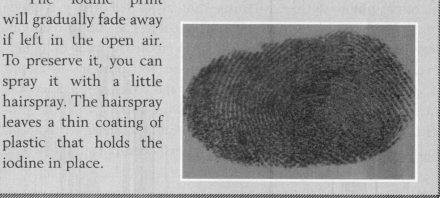

An important part of a scientist's work goes a step beyond the scientific method. Discovering a new bit of knowledge is of little use to anyone but the discoverer unless it is published. And then the publication can lead to other scientists retesting the hypothesis to make sure the original work was done properly and without errors. It can also lead to alternative hypotheses to explain the data and the experimental results, leading to new hypotheses and tests to see what is really going on.

In chemistry, this general scientific approach to learning new information is used all the time. So chemists are scientists. But so are mechanics, judges, animal trainers, and parents. Anyone who uses the scientific method can be a scientist.

How is physics different from chemistry?

Chemistry deals with matter. Physics also deals with matter—its motion, energy, and force. There is an obvious overlap between the two, especially in areas such as quantum chemistry and physical chemistry.

You can do a lot of chemistry without thinking much about the underlying physics. Mixing hydrochloric acid and sodium hydroxide will always give you salt water. Understanding why they react is important, and it is based on physics, but once you know why, you can rise above the physics and use the rules of chemistry to build new molecules or analyze crime-scene data without using our understanding of particle physics.

Some physicists like to think that all of chemistry is physics, since physics determines everything that goes on in reactions between molecules. But that would be to ignore the value of higher-level abstractions. A chemist can understand proteins as chains of amino acids, forming strings, sheets, and corkscrew shapes that interact to control the shape, and thus the function, of the protein. To try to understand protein synthesis by starting with quarks and photons would be to make it needlessly complicated. It would be like trying to understand a hurricane through its individual air molecules. If what you need is a rain forecast, higher-level abstractions will get you there with a lot less trouble.

The parts of physics that are not chemistry are huge. All of high-energy physics, the study of what goes on inside nuclei, the study of gravity, and things like relativity are all physics.

How are technology and chemistry different and alike?

Technology is about making and using tools. Sometimes the tools are physical things, and sometimes they are processes or systems that allow us to do something in a better way.

Chemists use many tools, so they use technology all the time. They use tools such as scales, spectrographs, gas chromatographs, mass spectrometers, computers, pH meters, and Bunsen burners. But they also use techniques such as titration, crystallization, chromatography, and flame tests, all of which are technologies, even if they don't use a particular tool.

Chemists are also at the forefront of tool design, helping design new materials for things like jet engines, surgical devices, lights, lasers, computer chips, and automobile engines.

Chemists are helping to develop new technologies all the time. New high-temperature superconductors are being made by chemists working with physicists. New kinds of rubber for car tires, new kinds of plastics for lightweight aircraft, biodegradable plastics for disposable eating utensils, and nanomaterials for electronics and medicine are just a few examples.

What does math have to do with chemistry?

Chemists use mathematics. Sometimes they use simple arithmetic to balance chemical equations. For example, we know that burning hydrogen with oxygen makes water:

$$H_2 + O_2 \rightarrow H_2O$$

But that equation is wrong, since there is only one oxygen on the right side, but there were two on the left side. So we use arithmetic to balance the equation:

$$2 H_2 + O_2 \rightarrow 2 H_2O$$

Chemists use simple mathematics to deal with ratios and proportions, units and dimensions, and simple statistics. They plot graphs of their observations and results.

Chemists also use more advanced mathematics to deal with rates of change in chemical reactions, to find maximums and minimums, or to determine other extremes or inflection points.

While mathematics is used a lot in chemistry, most of the mathematics is fairly simple. The mathematics in physics is generally more involved, and in physical chemistry you might find higher mathematics used more often than in many of the other branches of chemistry. The nature of the problem is usually what determines the tools needed to solve it.

What chemicals would you see if you were in a chemistry lab?

You'd generally see a lot of water in use. Chemists are always washing up, diluting, dissolving, or cooling something with water.

Aside from that, the chemicals in use will depend on what the chemist is trying to do. In many chemistry labs a standard set of reagents is available, including acids, bases, indicators, solvents, oxidizers, and reducing agents.

A biochemical lab might have agar for making nutrient gels, various minerals for encouraging the growth of microbes under study, stains for DNA or for microscopic study, disinfectants, genetic material, and primers for DNA amplification. A polymer chemistry lab might have a variety of monomers, solvents, and catalysts. An atmospheric chemistry lab may have little or no use for chemicals in the lab at all, or it might have a wide variety of volatile compounds to study.

PROJECT: COPPER CATALYST

Materials

Protective goggles
Paper towel
Glass jar or similar glass container
1 tablespoon acetone (available at
   hardware stores)
1 foot of copper wire (available at hardware stores)
Pencil
Pliers or tongs
Gas kitchen stove

Adult supervision required

The catalytic converter used in cars with internal combustion engines uses platinum and palladium catalysts to combine unburned fuel with oxygen to produce carbon dioxide and water vapor. This prevents the unburned fuel from creating smog. At the same time, the catalysts break down nitrogen oxides that also contribute to air pollution.

The converter needs to be hot in order to work, but once it starts working, the reaction provides extra heat to keep the catalyst hot. It actually glows red hot in use.

In this project, you are going to perform a similar catalytic reaction, but instead of using expensive noble metals like platinum and palladium, you will use simple copper wire as the catalyst. The drawback to using copper is that it is only able to catalyze a small number of fuels, such as methanol and acetone. But acetone is easy to come by at your local hardware store.

Start by *putting on protective goggles*. Curl up a strip of paper towel use it to line the sides of a glass jar as shown.

Then drop in about a tablespoon of acetone. The paper towel ensures that a lot of acetone vapor stays in the jar. You also need approximately 1 foot of copper wire, bent into a hook on one end and coiled up on the other end as shown, and a pencil from which to hang the wire. Make sure the wire will fit nicely in the jar.

Since the catalyst needs to be hot for the reaction to happen, use pliers or tongs to hold the wire in the flame of a gas stove until it is red hot and glowing.

The last step is to hang the glowing copper coil from the pencil so that the coil hangs in the center of the jar.

The copper coil gets even hotter than it was before we put it in the jar, as the acetone vapor and oxygen combine on the

surface of the copper, releasing heat. There is no flame, since the vapor is not actually burning. It is hot, however, and the copper glows yellow and white. You can feel the heat rising from the jar if you put your hand over it.

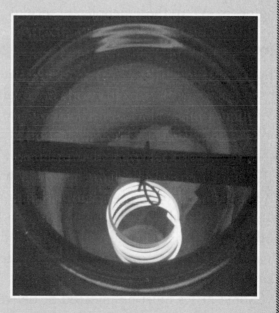

The reaction will last as long as there is acetone vapor to consume. The tablespoon of acetone I used in this project lasted several minutes, and the coil glowed hot enough to read by in the dark.

Why are chemists so serious about their work?

Some aren't. Chemists have a sense of humor like everyone else. I think.

Most chemists I know have a lot of fun doing chemistry, and they got into chemistry because they were having fun. But most people take their work seriously, especially if it can change the world and improve people's lives.

If your job was to create new molecules to cure a disease or to understand how human activities are affecting the environment or to figure out how to clean up nuclear waste, you would want to do a good job. But if you were a comedian or a circus clown, you would still want to do a good job. Most people take their jobs seriously.

Chemists must also be very careful when they work, so as not to injure themselves or others and to make sure that the results they get are correct. In this regard they are similar to firefighters and accountants, soldiers and rocket scientists, and doctors and engineers. All of those people are serious about their work too.

How do you use chemistry in a pharmacy?

Pharmacies deal with medicines, and most medical compounds are small organic molecules, such as aspirin or ethanol, or larger biological molecules, mostly proteins like insulin or prolactin. So a pharmacist is doing a fair bit of chemistry, in addition to biology, medicine, and retail sales.

Pharmacists are not just concerned with how their chemicals affect the body of the patient, but they are also concerned with how the molecules interact with one another, how they affect the body in combination, and how they are delivered. To make a pill that survives the stomach acid and is delivered into the intestines can be complicated.

Some drugs must be injected or delivered through the skin in some other way, because they can't pass through the digestive tract unaltered. Most proteins are in this category. Some are inhaled for

PROJECT: HOLLOW PENNIES

Materials

Stack of pennies minted after 1982
Metal file, nail file, or emery board
2 teaspoons salt
½ cup vinegar
Water
Thread or wire, long enough to make a necklace
Muriatic acid (optional, available at hardware stores and swimming
    pool supply houses)
Protective goggles (optional)

In 1982 the US Mint stopped using 95 percent copper for pennies and switched to a cheaper design, made of zinc coated with a thin layer of copper.

In the photo on the right I have a stack of pennies from after 1982, each of which has had a bit of the copper plating filed off the edges. I filed each penny on opposite sides, so the zinc shows through on the top and the bottom edges. If I could remove the zinc from inside, leaving only the paper-thin copper, I could string these hollow penny shells on a string to make a necklace.

As it turns out, you can. Many acids will react with zinc but not with copper. One such acid is hydrochloric acid. You can make a weak (and safe) form by combining about ½ cup of vinegar with about 2 teaspoons of salt (as much as will dissolve in the vinegar). You'll have to wait a day or two for it to do the trick, though. For a much faster reaction, you can use a stronger form of hydrochloric acid called muriatic acid, available at hardware stores and swimming pool supply houses. When handling muriatic acid, *always use eye protection*, and make sure you have *adult supervision*.

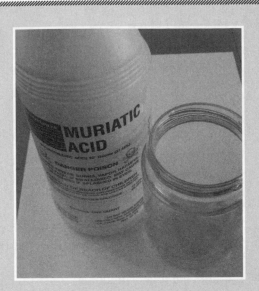

Of course, I chose the faster method. Here you can see hydrogen bubbling up from the filed pennies as the exposed zinc reacts with the acid.

The acid also cleans off any tarnish from the copper. As it reacts with the tarnish, more hydrogen is released, and you can see that while most of the bubbles are coming from the filed-off places, there is still some coming from the rest of the penny as the tarnish reacts with the acid.

After a few hours, the pennies will float to the top of the acid

and stop bubbling. They float because they are thin copper shells of their former selves and they are filled with hydrogen.

Now you can add a lot of water to the jar to dilute the acid, and it can be safely poured down the sink. Rinse the pennies well, and then you can string them on a thread or a wire to make a necklace.

A close-up view shows the penny is actually hollow.

the same reason or because they act faster that way. Knowing how chemistry affects drug delivery is an important part of designing pills, capsules, injectables, and inhalants.

Many drugs act on the body in similar ways, and when used in combination, they can have harmful effects. Pills that make you drowsy are generally not safe to take when drinking alcohol, for example. The alcohol can increase the effects or side effects of the drug, and the drug can increase the effects of the alcohol.

In other cases, a drug might cause the body to produce an enzyme that breaks down another drug the patient might be taking. Understanding chemistry allows the pharmacist to suggest that the pills be taken at different times or that another drug be substituted for one of the originals.

How do doctors use chemistry in their work?

Your doctor knows a surprising amount of chemistry. The chemistry of blood or urine or even of your breath can all tell her something about your health. She may suggest chemicals to alter some chemical process in your body, such as statin drugs to lower your cholesterol, or vitamins to make your body function properly.

Your body is a vast chemical processing plant, and much of what medicine is about is concerned with how the body produces and uses chemicals. Even when the doctor is just sewing up a cut on a finger, she might be thinking about the chemistry of blood coagulation, the brain chemistry of pain, and how aspirin might affect both of them.

Doctors use chemistry to control infections, both by washing themselves, their tools, and their patients with disinfectants and by giving the patient chemicals that attack bacteria without harming the patient's tissues.

The adhesive on a Band-Aid was designed by a chemist. So was the plastic it was made from.

A doctor might need to recognize the symptoms of poisoning caused by chemical exposure or drug overdoses. Even more understanding of chemistry helps her repair or mitigate the damage by absorbing or neutralizing the poison or by helping the body heal afterward.

One of the doctors most concerned with chemistry is the anesthesiologist, the doctor who controls your state of consciousness during surgery. He needs to know the effects of oxygen and the many drugs at his disposal and how to monitor the patient for signs of trouble.

How is chemistry used in cooking?

All of the ingredients used in the kitchen are chemicals, and almost all of the techniques used in cooking are concerned with chemical changes in the food you prepare.

The baking powder you use to make pancakes rise is a good example. Sodium bicarbonate powder supplies the carbon dioxide bubbles, and dry acid salts such as tartaric acid and monocalcium phosphate are used to release it by reacting with the bicarbonate. These reactions take place as soon as water is added to the dry powder. Other acid salts such as sodium aluminum sulfate are also added, since these only react at higher temperatures in the oven or on the griddle. This allows the batter to still rise after it has been sitting on the counter for a while.

A chemist knows that green vegetables turn an ugly drab color when the magnesium atom at the center of the chlorophyll molecule is replaced by a hydrogen atom. This can happen when green vegetables are heated or when an acid is present. Cooking for a shorter time or avoiding acids like vinegar or lemon juice can keep the colors bright.

Knowing what temperatures change the structure of the proteins in food can also be extremely helpful in cooking. Each of the proteins in an egg, for example, hardens at a different temperature. If you can keep your egg at a temperature at which all of the white hardens but little or none of the yolk does, you can have very tight control over how your eggs are cooked.

Controlling the temperature while meat cooks is important for the same reason. If you never allow your meat to reach the temperature at which the meat proteins harden, you can avoid a tough cut, while allowing a high enough temperature to convert all of the tough connective tissue into soft gelatin.

10

Food

Everyone loves to eat, and *needs* to eat. Our bodies are made of chemicals, and we need new chemicals to fuel us, build the parts that grow, and rebuild the parts that are constantly wearing out. Chemicals are what make food look, smell, and taste the way they do. They are what make food healthy and good for us. We tend to forget about all the good chemicals in food because we fear the ones that are bad for us or that we don't understand. But knowledge of food chemistry can alleviate that fear.

Why are some foods made with chemicals?

Of course all food is made from chemicals. But this book has discussed the meaning of the word *chemical* earlier and found that people without a scientific education confuse the word *chemical* with concepts such as things in my oatmeal you can't pronounce.

Oatmeal is a wonderful food all by itself. The Fruit & Maple Oatmeal you get at McDonald's might have far too much sugar added, but that is not the "chemical" that people are complaining about, even if it is the most dangerous ingredient in the bowl.

The oatmeal contains rolled oats, brown sugar, modified food starch (regular starch broken down into smaller molecules to change its thickness), salt, natural flavor (from plant sources—specifically the maple flavor), barley malt extract (what you put in malted milk), and caramel color (burned sugar).

The diced apples in the oatmeal are made from apples and have calcium ascorbate added as an antioxidant to keep the color from changing. Calcium is an essential nutrient, and ascorbate is vitamin C. Many people think antioxidants are good for your health and that we should get more of them.

The cranberry raisin blend includes cranberries and raisins—and more sugar. It also has sunflower oil, and the dried fruit has been preserved with sulfur dioxide. Most dried fruit you eat is preserved this way. Some people are sensitive to sulfites, which are formed by the preservative, but most of the sulfur dioxide has dissipated by the time the product gets to the consumer.

The light cream part of the product has the most unfamiliar names. Milk and cream are in it, but so are sodium phosphate, diacetyl tartaric ester of monoglyceride, sodium stearoyl lactylate, sodium citrate, and carrageenan.

Sodium phosphate is one of the electrolytes added to sports drinks. It controls the acidity and stabilizes the proteins in the milk. Datem (diacetyl tartaric ester of monoglyceride) is an emulsifier made from vegetable oil and cream of tartar, which keeps the cream from separating from the milk. Sodium stearoyl lactylate is another emulsifying agent. Sodium citrate is a salt of citric acid (the stuff in orange juice), and it prevents milk from curdling by acting as an acid buffering agent, much like sodium phosphate. Carrageenan is a thickening agent (like a starch) that is made from seaweed.

With these ingredients the milk can be stored and transported without curds and lumps of fat forming. You will find these ingredients in single-serving coffee creamers for the same reason.

Why do we need calcium?

Your bones are made from calcium phosphate. So are your teeth. But your body uses calcium in other tissues, such as muscles, the heart, and the nerves.

When you are growing, your bones need to grow, and so you need calcium. If you get regular exercise, your bones feel the forces and respond by adding calcium phosphate to become stronger. If you do not get enough exercise, the bones weaken and can break more easily.

When your body needs calcium for the muscles and nerves, it can get it by dissolving bone tissue to get more calcium into the bloodstream. You will gradually lose calcium from your bones if you do not get more calcium in your diet. You also need vitamin D in order to process and absorb calcium from your food.

Most bone building occurs when you are young. Later in life, your body will use the calcium you stored in your bones when you were growing. In older people, and especially in women, the loss of calcium can make the bones weak and brittle. So it is important to get plenty of calcium, vitamin D, and exercise when you are young. Your body is banking calcium.

As you get older, less calcium is needed, since your bones are not growing. But getting adequate calcium to replace what is lost is still important, as is exercise and vitamin D.

Calcium is an element, so your body cannot make it but must get it from the environment. Besides vitamin D, other things that help absorb calcium from the diet are protein, magnesium, and phosphorus. Some foods, such as spinach, sugar, alcohol, and coffee, can prevent calcium absorption.

An adult woman has about two pounds of calcium in her body. An adult man has about three pounds. All but 1 percent of it is in the bones.

Calcium helps muscles contract, helps blood clot, controls blood pressure, and helps prevent gum disease. Lack of calcium can cause leg cramps, muscle spasms, and nerve sensitivity.

Why do we need to eat food?

You eat food because your hormones tell you to. It is obvious that in order to grow, a body needs to accumulate the material out of which it is made. But adults who have stopped growing (at least vertically) still lose mass every day and must replace it.

But you also eat in order to get energy. You eat fats and carbohydrates mostly for the energy they provide. You can also burn proteins, but you mostly eat proteins to get the raw materials for making the proteins that our body is made from and that you use as catalysts (enzymes) to guide chemical reactions.

But the urge to eat, that need you feel when you are hungry, is due to hormones. The hormone *ghrelin* is produced in the brain but also in the pancreas and the lining of the stomach. It is produced at high levels before meals and decreases after meals. It makes you feel hungry.

Other molecules that make you feel hungry are *neuropeptide Y*, which is secreted by your intestines, and *anandamide*.

Another hormone, *leptin*, is produced in fat cells. It makes you feel full. It affects your appetite and also how fast you burn energy. It acts by inhibiting the effects of neuropeptide Y and anandamide and increasing levels of α-MSH (alpha MSH), which is another appetite suppressant.

Other hormones and signaling molecules (such as *insulin*) are involved in regulating appetite and metabolism, and each of the hormones and signals are used in different places in the body to do different things. The science of how we regulate our metabolism is very complex and interrelated with other bodily functions in complicated ways.

How does chemistry keep your food safe?

Understanding the chemistry of how foods go bad allows us to design countermeasures to prevent spoilage. Some of those countermeasures involve knowing what kills bacteria and molds and what causes food to break down all by itself.

Living things need enzymes to do their job. Enzymes are proteins that use their particular shape to guide chemical reactions. If something changes that shape from its natural form, it is called *denaturing* the protein. A denatured enzyme usually does not work properly.

One way to denature enzymes is to heat them. When food is sealed in cans and then heated, all of the enzymes inside are denatured. That kills the bacteria and molds, since they need their enzymes to survive. And it also denatures the enzymes in the food, which would otherwise cause the food to break down into an unappetizing mush. It is enzymes that cause fruit to bruise and meat to spoil.

Bacteria and mold can also be prevented from growing by using chemicals. There are two classes of chemicals that prevent bacteria and molds from producing the energy they need to live and grow. These are the benzoates and the propionates.

In acidic foods, benzoic acid or sodium benzoate can be used to keep bacteria and molds from spoiling the food. Benzoic acid and benzoates are found naturally in dried fruit, and they may be a natural antibiotic in those fruits. They prevent the microbes from fermenting sugar into alcohol.

Benzoates only work in acidic foods. Calcium propionate is used in foods that are not acidic, such as baked goods. Higher forms of life can metabolize propionates, but in bacteria and mold the molecule interferes with energy production.

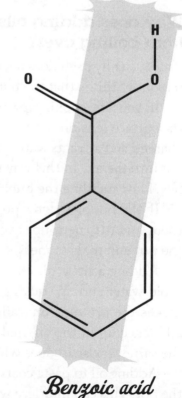

Benzoic acid

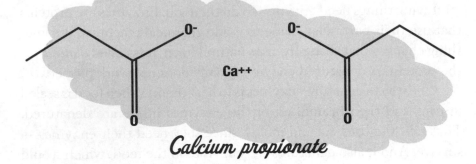

Calcium propionate

There are many other molecules that harm bacteria and molds but not people and animals and are thus used to preserve food. In addition to those, molecules like salt and alcohol can be used in large quantities to kill germs but then be rinsed off before the food is consumed.

Why does adding oils to cooking water keep it from boiling over?

Plain water by itself does not usually boil over the edge of the pot. The reason for this is that the bubbles pop when they reach the surface.

If you are cooking pasta, the proteins from the pasta change the surface tension of the water. Proteins often have one side that is charged and attracts water and another side that is not, which sticks out into the air. In this way proteins act like the soap in a soap bubble. They stabilize the bubble, so it can live longer before popping.

If the bubbles don't pop, then new bubbles form underneath them and lift them up. Eventually they will spill over the edge of the pot and make a mess.

Adding a little oil changes this. The ends of the proteins that avoid water end up sticking into the oil instead of into the air. This makes the proteins unavailable to stabilize the bubbles. They are all locked up in the oil, making tiny oil droplets out of bigger ones, the same way soap does when you wash the dishes.

Adding oil to pasta coats the pasta with oil when you lift it out of the pot. This can interfere with the sauces, so they no longer coat the noodles. You can pour out the surface water first, so the oil goes down the drain, or you can stop putting oil in the pasta and just watch the pot more carefully. If you turn down the heat when the water starts to boil over, you can prevent the mess without chemistry.

As long as the water is boiling at all, it will be at the temperature of boiling water. Boiling the water faster only makes the water evaporate faster. It does not speed up the cooking, since the temperature cannot get higher than the boiling point as long as there is still water in the pot.

Why do onions make you cry?

Because of 1-Sulfinylpropane.

This inconvenient little molecule is produced by enzymes in the onion when you cut it. Normally these enzymes are locked up inside the onion cells, but the knife breaks open the cells and lets the enzymes out, where they react with other molecules that arc released, making 1-Sulfinylpropane.

Since 1-Sulfinylpropane is a small molecule, it can easily evaporate into the air. It gets into your nose and eyes, where the sensors in the eye that protect it from harmful substances get alerted. To flush out the bad molecules, the eyes and nose produce large amounts of liquid in an attempt to wash away the irritant.

Some onions produce less of this molecule than others. Onions grown in low-sulfur soils generally produce less, and there are sweet onions like the Vidalia that produce less of it.

1-Sulfinylpropane

You can prevent the tears in a number of ways. You can chill the onion in the refrigerator before cutting it. Enzymes work more slowly when they are cold. You can chop the onions under a fan, so the molecule never gets to your eyes and nose. You can chop the onion underwater (although just how practical does that sound?). You can wear your protective chemistry goggles, the ones that make a tight seal around your eyes. Or you can use a nice little onion-chopping gadget that chops them under a plastic container.

How do you make rock candy?

Rock candy is crystallized sugar. The crystals are usually grown slowly (over a week or two) to get large, attractive crystals. Growing crystals quickly makes a mass of small crystals instead of nice large crystals.

To get the crystals to grow slowly, you need to control the rate at which the sugar precipitates out of a sugar solution. If you boil the water out of the solution quickly, you get candy like taffy or nougat, where the crystals are so tiny you can't feel them on your tongue. If you disturb the candy by beating it, you also get billions of tiny crystals, as you do when you make fudge.

To make rock candy crystals, start with plain sugar and water. Two cups of sugar will dissolve in one cup of water if you boil the water. If you want to make more candy, you can double the recipe.

Boil the sugar and water together until all the sugar dissolves. Remove the pan from the heat. At this point you can add food coloring or flavors like vanilla, mint, cherry, lemon, grape, or strawberry. Let the liquid cool for at least 10 minutes.

Next, take some string or some wooden skewers and dip them into the liquid. You can let the liquid dry on the string to form seed crystals, or you can roll them in granulated sugar and let them sit to dry for a bit. Drying allows the crystals to form in the crevices of the string or wood, so they are well anchored.

Fill some jars with the remaining liquid.

Now hang the string or skewers in the jars, being careful to keep them above the bottom of the jar. Crystals will form on the strings or skewers, but they will also form at the bottom of the jar and at the surface of the liquid. If the string or skewer touches the bottom, the rock candy crystals on the string will join those at the bottom, and you will get a big mass that you can't remove.

I like to put the jars into saucers of water so they don't attract ants. I also cover them with paper so that flies aren't attracted to the syrup. After a week, as the water slowly evaporates, the sugar will be forced out of solution and will crystallize on surfaces in the jar, such as the string or wood, that were seeded with small sugar crystals. Crystals grow first where there are already seed crystals.

Grow your crystals for 7 to 14 days and remove them when they are the size you like. As crystals form at the surface of the syrup, you can knock them down into the jar or remove them.

The biggest crystals will grow in a cool solution that is placed in a location free of vibrations from running feet or slamming doors.

Why does salt have a texture?

Because salt is made of tiny crystals in the shape of cubes.

Salt is made of sodium and chlorine. Chlorine atoms are a little bigger than sodium atoms. Chlorine is 181 picometers in radius, and sodium is only 102 picometers. They have opposite charges, so they pack as closely as they can, given their different sizes. That turns out to be the shape of a cube.

The salt in your salt shaker may have been ground up from larger crystals, so many of the crystals may be broken, especially if you have a salt grinder instead of a salt shaker. But many salt companies crystallize their salt to purify it and arrange the conditions of the crystallization so that perfectly sized little cubes are formed.

You can use a magnifying glass or a microscope to see the tiny cube shapes. Or you can dissolve as much salt as you can in boiling water and let some of it slowly evaporate in a glass dish. If the evaporation rate is slow (because you let the solution cool in the

Sodium chloride crystal structure

refrigerator) you will get larger cubes that you can see without a magnifying glass.

Why is chocolate a solid?

Remember the talk about why ice and snow melt (page 169)? The same processes (of equilibrium at a given temperature) occur in most materials. When the temperature rises above the melting point, molecules leave the solid and enter the liquid at a faster rate than the molecules in the liquid crystallize onto the solid.

The fat in cocoa beans (called cocoa butter) melts in a narrow temperature range, between 93° and 100° Fahrenheit (34° to 38° Celsius). Normal human body temperature is in this range. So if the temperature is hot enough to melt chocolate, your body has a hard time staying cool, and you move into the shade. So chocolate is a solid because you live in a comfortable place.

Part of what we like in chocolate is that it is a solid in the wrapper on the table but becomes a soft paste or liquid in the mouth.

Other fats have different melting points. Tristearin is a hard, waxy fat that melts at 154° Fahrenheit (68° Celsius). Triolein, which has three kinks in the molecule, so it can't form compact crystals as easily as tristearin, melts at 41° Fahrenheit (5° Celsius).

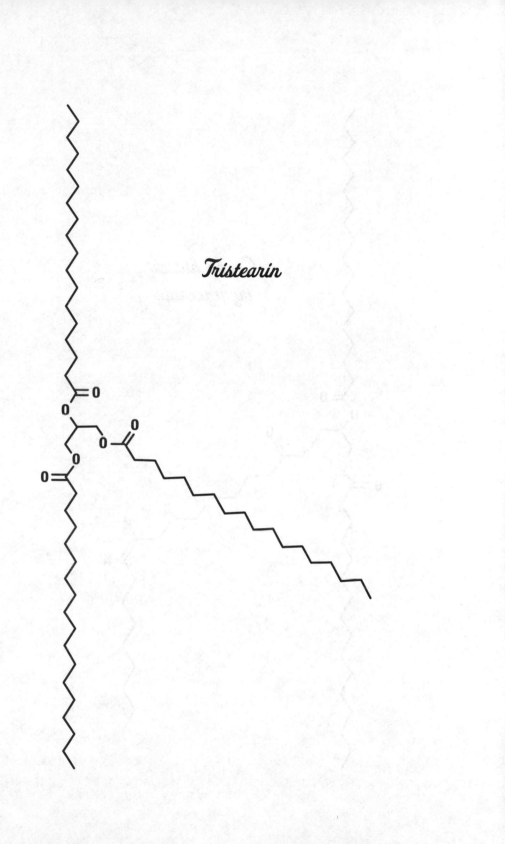

Tristearin

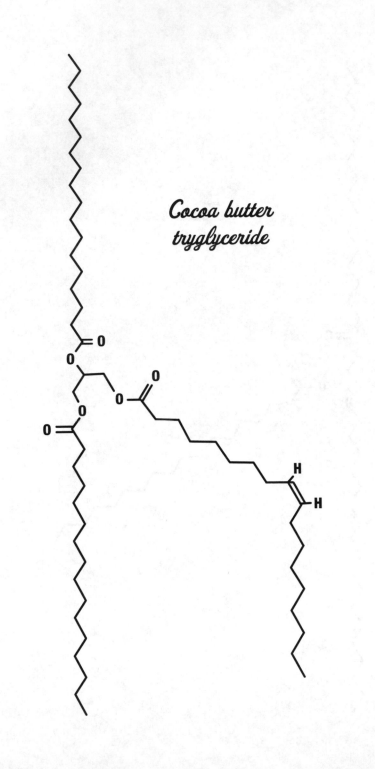

Cocoa butter tryglyceride

Cocoa butter has a mix of fats but is made mostly from the fatty acids stearic acid, palmitic acid, and oleic acid, sometimes on the same glycerin molecule, as shown on the previous page.

This arrangement gives it a melting point in between that of the solid tristearin and the triolein, which is liquid at room temperature. So our chocolate bar stays solid as long as we don't leave it out in the sun.

Why is peanut butter creamy?

Well, some types are chunky. But disregarding the larger bits of peanut in your peanut butter, the creamy texture of it is due to the fact that peanuts are mostly made of peanut oil.

The peanut butter you get in the store is made of very finely ground peanuts, so your tongue cannot feel the individual particles. They are surrounded by peanut oil, which is a liquid. The fine peanut flour absorbs the oil, and the result is a thick paste.

Of course peanut butter does not resemble cream in either color or consistency. The producers of peanut butter call it creamy because that sounds better than pasty.

Peanut butter contains very little moisture. In your mouth, it takes a while to eat peanut butter because you have to moisten it before you can swallow.

Are there chemicals in artificial flavors?

Yes. But of course, there are chemicals in natural flavors too . . . usually the same ones that are in artificial flavors.

A common artificial flavor is vanillin. Natural vanilla flavoring is a mixture of hundreds of different flavor molecules, but the most prevalent molecule in it is vanillin. Since vanillin can be synthesized much more cheaply than it can be extracted from vanilla beans, the synthetic form is much more widely available.

A more potent form of the molecule is ethyl vanillin. Both of these synthetic molecules are used to add flavor to foods such as chocolate, where the subtle differences between the natural and

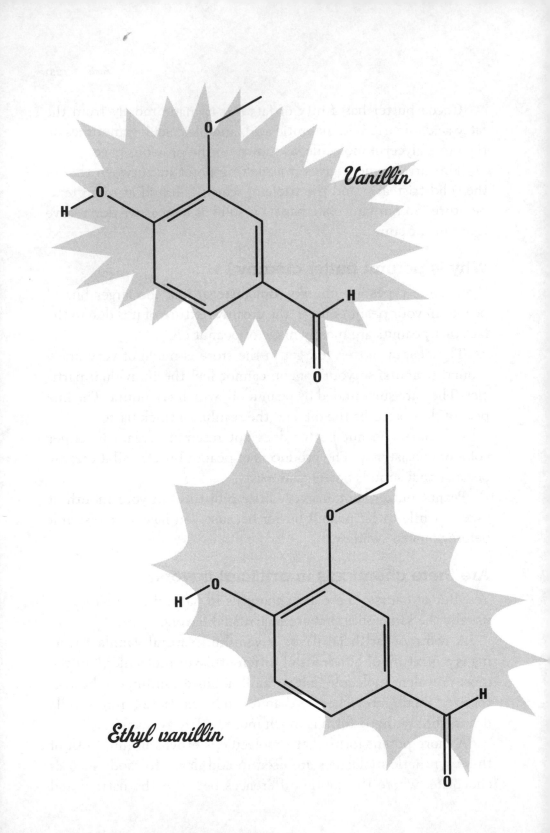

Vanillin

Ethyl vanillin

the synthetic molecules would be lost among all of the other strong flavors.

Many other artificial flavors have been synthesized. Most of them are esters, a compound made from an alcohol and an organic acid. As with vanillin, these molecules are the same ones found as the principal flavorings in natural flavors. For example, isoamyl acetate is the main molecule that gives bananas their flavor and aroma.

Octyl acetate is the main flavor component in oranges.

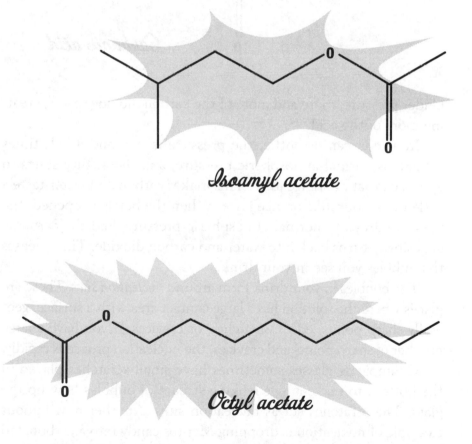

Isoamyl acetate

Octyl acetate

What makes soda so fizzy?

Carbonic acid.

Actually, when carbon dioxide is dissolved in water, only a small portion of it reacts with the water to form carbonic acid.

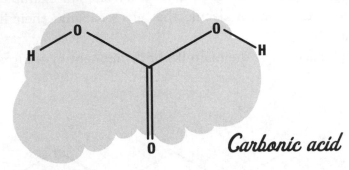

Carbonic acid

Under pressure, more and more of the carbon dioxide reacts, creating more of the acid.

In a soda can or bottle, the pressure is two and a half times as high as normal atmospheric pressure, and the acidity starts to approach that of orange juice. This makes carbonated water taste a little tart—sour, like orange juice. When the bottle is opened, the pressure drops to normal atmospheric pressure, and the carbonic acid slowly turns back into water and carbon dioxide. This releases the bubbles you see in your drink.

The bubbles in your drink form around *nucleation sites*. These are places where the solution has a large contact area with a surface, generally sharp points, edges, scratches, or crevices. If you have a large number of sharp points and crevices, the nucleation proceeds rapidly.

Champagne glasses sometimes have small scratches placed in the bottom to make a nice looking stream of bubbles flow up the glass. The scratches act as nucleation sites. Another now-famous example of nucleation is dropping Mentos candy into a carbonated beverage and watching the rapid, almost violent release of carbon dioxide from the millions of nucleation sites the candy offers.

PROJECT: DANCING RAISINS

Materials

Dried blueberries
Dried cherries

Raisins
Flavored sparkling water

Sometimes an extremely simple demonstration can stimulate quite a bit of thought.

I had my assistant drop some dried blueberries, dried cherries, and raisins into a glass of flavored sparkling water. They all quickly sank to the bottom, surrounded by a cloud of bubbles. After a short while, the raisins began to float up. When they reached the top, they sank back down to the bottom again, to start the process all over. They looked like wrinkled little submarines, bobbing up and down.

But the dried cherries and dried blueberries just sat there at the bottom.

The questions began very soon. What makes them go up? What makes them fall down again? Why do only the raisins seem to be active?

The carbonic acid in the soda water is slowly converting to water and carbon dioxide gas, because it is no longer under high pressure in the can. The easiest way for the gas to leave the water is at the water's surface. Making a new bubble from scratch takes more energy than simply enlarging an existing bubble.

At the top of the glass is a large surface open to the air. Most of the carbon dioxide gas escapes at that large surface. But as the dried fruit was dropped into the soda, bubbles of air were trapped in the wrinkled surface of the fruit. These bubbles of air act as extra surfaces, and the carbon dioxide gas escapes into them, making the bubbles bigger. When the bubbles are big enough, they rise to the surface. If they are stuck to a raisin, they can lift the raisin to the surface with them.

Once the raisin is at the surface, the bubbles continue to grow, and they either detach from the raisin or they pop (since they are now at the surface). In either case, the raisin no longer has enough gas to keep it afloat, and it falls back down. Usually the bubble that popped or detached left a tiny remnant of itself stuck to the raisin, and that tiny bubble starts to grow again.

But why did the dried cherries stay at the bottom?

The cherries are much like the raisins, but they are larger. This makes something interesting happen. Imagine a box just big enough to hold a marble. It has one marble in it, and it has six sides that can collect bubbles like the raisin. Now imagine that we double the width, height, and depth of the box, so that eight marbles can fit into it. The box now has eight times the weight but only four times the surface area to collect bubbles. Now there aren't enough bubbles to lift the weight. The dried cherries are just too big for the bubbles on the surface to lift.

But the small dried blueberries also stayed at the bottom. Why is that?

We looked closely at the blueberries. The bubbles there seemed to leave the surface of the blueberry before they got big enough to float it. It looked as though the surface of the berry was not as sticky to the bubbles as the surfaces of the other fruits. The blueberries also seemed to be a little denser than the other fruits, so there was more weight for each bubble to lift. Something about the surface of the blueberries seemed to be the most important thing, though. They just didn't have as many small trapped bubbles as the other fruits. It was like they were smoother or covered in a soap-like substance that allowed the water to wet them better.

All of this from a simple glass of soda and some dried fruit. Who would have thought?

Why do people tap on soda cans before they open them?

Not everyone does. But the idea is to release the gas bubbles that have nucleated on the inside surface of the can, so the bubbles float to the top and pop.

If there are numerous bubbles already formed on the inside of the can, when the pressure in the can is released, these bubble grow in size immediately, becoming many times their previous size. At the same time, they act as surface area for more carbon dioxide gas to form, making the bubble bigger still.

If enough of the now-large bubbles form low in the can, they make the contents of the can (the soda inside) increase in volume, causing it to spill out of the can. If the top of the can has not been quickly and fully opened, a stream of bubbly soda can shoot out of the narrow opening, making a sticky mess, usually in the direction of the person opening the can.

Tapping on the can or setting it on the table with a thump will dislodge the bubbles from the inner side of the can, where they accumulate at the top and break. Now when the can is opened, only the gas escapes from the initially small opening. The gas makes much less of a mess when it hits the face of the person looking for a cool drink.

What are all of the chemicals in soda?

Besides carbonic acid and water, soda water often contains sodium compounds such as sodium bicarbonate (baking soda), which are slightly alkaline. The alkaline salts counteract the acidity of the carbonated water and make it taste slightly salty, like the mineral water it was originally made to resemble. It is these sodium salts that give soda its name.

In flavored sodas, sugar or other sweeteners change how the tongue reacts to the acid, in the same way that adding sugar to lemon juice makes lemonade taste far less sour than the lemon. In fact, so much sugar is added that additional acids are needed to add the refreshing hint of tartness we like. This is why many soft drinks (especially colas) add phosphoric acid to the drink. Citric acid is also often added, especially in citrus-flavored drinks. Another common additive for tartness is malic acid, the molecule that makes apples tart.

Benzoic acid or sodium benzoate is often added, since it prevents bacteria and molds from being able to ferment sugars and spoil the flavors in the drink.

To maintain the levels of acidity, a buffering agent such as sodium phosphate is sometimes added. This keeps the acidity at a fixed level, so the product tastes the same all the time, even as the carbonic acid levels get low as the carbon dioxide bubbles form and break.

Caffeine is often added as a stimulant drug. Naturally present in cola and other plant-derived flavorings (and in coffee and tea), caffeine was one of the main reasons to drink cola drinks when they were first invented.

Caramel color and FD&C colors are also added to many soft drinks, just to make them look more appetizing.

Does bottled water go bad?

No. Many bottled waters have an expiration date on them. This is not because they will go bad but because some places have laws that say every drink has to have an expiration date. Even if you don't live in such a place, the bottling company wants to be able to sell the water in those places, so they print a date on the bottle. It may also help their sales if people think they have to buy new bottles of water instead of drinking the older ones in the back of the refrigerator.

Plastic bottles will gradually release volatile molecules from the plastic. Most of these will escape into the air, but some of them will get into the water. It is unlikely that you would be able to taste them in the water, however, and it is not clear that they would accumulate over time instead of being reabsorbed in the plastic once they reach equilibrium levels in the water. Glass bottles don't have volatile molecules to leach into the water.

An unopened bottle will not allow algae or bacteria to grow in it. Once the bottle has been opened, however, it is possible that algae spores could make their way into it, and with enough sunlight, you could get a green film on the inside of the bottle.

What makes cookies rise?

The same carbon dioxide bubbles that make sodas fizzy make cookies rise. In bread, those carbon dioxide bubbles are made by yeast, a tiny microbe that eats sugar and makes alcohol and carbon dioxide. In cookies, the bubbles are formed by a reaction between baking soda (sodium bicarbonate) and an acid.

The acid can be from something tart in the recipe, such as lemon juice or other fruit juices, vinegar, or buttermilk. Or it can be an acid produced when water is added to powdered tartaric acid (cream of tartar) or monocalcium phosphate. These are the powders that, along with baking soda, make baking powder.

Baking soda by itself will decompose to release carbon dioxide as the temperature of the cookie rises. Steam will also enter the bubbles and expand them. Air that was beaten into the cookie dough will also expand as the cookies get hot. All of these things combine to help make the cookies rise in the oven.

When the cookies cool, however, those hot gases will contract again. If the cookie has not been chemically changed by the heat, it will fall and get flat again. The chemical changes in the cookie that help it keep its fluffy texture and shape after it cools are mostly reactions of proteins. As proteins are heated, their carefully formed three-dimensional structures unwind (denature), and the untangled strings and sheets of protein can form bonds with other proteins. The proteins join up into big nets and sheets that hold the bubbles in place, and as the hot gases cool and try to contract, the proteins hold their shape, so air from the outside is sucked in.

Why does a white of an egg turn white when you cook it?

The same protein denaturing that keeps cookies fluffy happens when you cook an egg. The white of an egg is a transparent gel before cooking. The proteins are dissolved in water, but they have electrical charges on their surfaces that make them repel one another. This gives the liquid its gel form and keeps much of the egg white in a high puddle around the egg yolk.

There are several different proteins in the egg white. Some are more gelled than others. If you crack an egg, you will see a runny, almost watery protein solution on the outside, and a firmer gel of egg white toward the center.

As you heat the egg white, some of the proteins denature sooner than others (at a lower temperature). As the proteins unfold, the electrical charges that were on the inside are available to form bonds on the outside. The proteins take up more space as they get bigger and start to bond with one another.

These larger proteins scatter light more effectively than they did when all the molecules were smaller than a wavelength of visible light. Instead of a transparent gel, the egg proteins become as white as clouds, which scatter light in the same way. As the temperature rises, more of the proteins denature and bond together. The proteins in the yolk are the last to solidify, at the highest temperatures.

Why does jelly feel squishy?

Jelly feels squishy because of electricity. You just learned about the gel in an egg white, in which the proteins were kept separate by their electrical charges on the outside of the molecule. Jelly is made of water in which huge molecules are dissolved, much like the protein molecules in egg white.

The molecules in jelly that make it firm are made of sugars that are all bonded together into huge, tangled molecules made of many thousands of sugar units. Unlike starch, which is somewhat similar but made of only the sugar glucose, pectins contain several different kinds of sugars. Plants use pectins as building materials, to give shape and strength to their cell walls.

Pectins react to heat in a way that is almost the opposite of proteins. Whereas proteins unfold and connect to one another as the temperature rises, pectins do not. Instead, as the temperature gets warmer, the pectins bounce around against one another more and lose their rigidity.

When fruit and fruit juices that contain pectin are heated, the pectins leave the cell walls and dissolve in the water around them. When the water cools, the pectins stop jostling and settle down next to one another but are still kept apart by their electrical charges. If there is enough sugar in the juice, the pectins firm up.

The result is a firm gel that you can poke, jiggle, and squish with your fingers or your tongue. The molecules are not strongly bound together, so the jelly is not a solid. But sugar and the large molecules of pectin lock up the water molecules around them, so they don't flow like water. The result is jelly.

How does a fruit get ripe?

Fruits are a way for plants to spread their seeds. To attract animals and birds to the seeds and get them to spread the seeds, the plant makes the fruit sweet, soft, and fragrant and usually changes the color to indicate that this fruit is ready to have its seeds scattered. Unripe fruits are not sweet, generally not fragrant, and remain a different color, so they are not picked before the seeds are ready.

During ripening, stored starches are converted to sugar. This makes the fruit sweet, and it also makes it softer. The pectin in the cell walls breaks down, further softening the fruit. The chlorophyll breaks down, allowing the yellows, reds, and oranges to show through. Anthocyanins are produced to get purples and reds, while also acting as sunscreens and antioxidants to keep the fruit tasting good.

The hormone that triggers ripening is a small molecule called ethylene. Commercial fruit growers sometimes pick the fruit (especially bananas) while it is still green and hard, so it can handle transportation without bruising. They then add ethylene gas to the containers of fruit to start the ripening process. By the time the fruit is in the market, it is nearly ripe.

Why is honey so sticky?

Hydrogen bonds make honey sticky. Earlier you learned about hydrogen bonds (page 153). Unlike other some bonds, hydrogen bonds form between molecules instead of between atoms in a compound. The attraction between honey and your fingers is due to hydrogen bonds in the honey attracting molecules in your fingers.

Honey is mostly water, fructose, and glucose. The last two are simple sugars, also known as monosaccharides. These three ingredients make up 86 percent of honey, with other sugars making up the bulk of the rest. Sugars bind well to water. Almost all of the 17 percent of honey that is water is bonded (with hydrogen bonds) to sugar, so that little water remains to support bacteria or molds. This is why honey needs no refrigeration.

The hydrogen bonds between the sugars and the water make the honey viscous, so it pours slowly and feels thick. Those same bonds make it stick to your fingers. But water also bonds to your fingers with hydrogen bonds but doesn't feel sticky. What is the difference?

When your fingers get wet, they do tend to stick to one another a little bit more than when they are dry. But water does not stick very well to itself, so when you pull your wet fingers apart, a little water remains on each finger. The water sticks to your fingers more than it sticks to itself.

Honey sticks to itself far more than water does. You can see this when you pour the two liquids out of a cup. The honey takes a long time to pour out.

When the honey sticks to your fingers, it also sticks to itself. You have to use more force to pull your fingers apart than if they were just wet with water. We call that feeling "sticky."

Why does butter melt?

You already know about why snow and ice melt (page 169) and why chocolate melts (page 228). Butter is similar, but a little bit different.

All of them melt when a rise in temperature shifts the equilibrium between melting and solidifying. Butter, like chocolate, contains a mixture of fats. But butter has a wider mix of different fats and doesn't melt at a particular temperature all at once. Butter softens over a range of temperatures, until finally a temperature is reached where it is almost entirely liquid.

Butter is different from ice in another way. Butter is an emulsion of tiny water droplets inside of the fat. Each droplet is completely surrounded by fat, and the fat forms a continuous coating over all of the water droplets. Like soap bubbles and the bubbles in bread and cookies, a *surfactant* molecule—in this case, milk protein—keeps one end in the water and the other end in the fat, stabilizing the droplet and preventing it from joining other droplets. This keeps the butter from separating into a layer of water and a layer of fat.

When the butter melts, the droplets are freed, and they do join together. You can see the layer of water under the layer of melted fat when you melt butter in a pot.

How do you make fake butter?

Fake butter, called margarine, is a bunch of tiny water droplets surrounded by a continuous coating of fat—just like butter. But the fat in this case comes from plants instead of a cow. Some early margarines used fat from beef, seals, whales, and fish, but modern margarine is mostly plant-based. Some butter substitutes mix in some cream from cows to make it taste more like butter.

As with butter, the emulsifying agent is milk proteins: skim milk. Vegetable fats tend to be unsaturated to some degree and thus have low melting points, making them oils. To raise the melting point, the oils are saturated with hydrogen using catalysts. This is called *hydrogenation,* and the result is hydrogenated vegetable oil.

Partially hydrogenated vegetable oils used to be used in margarine and butter substitutes, but when oils are heated in the process of hydrogenating, some harmful trans fats are produced. If the fat is fully hydrogenated, so that every carbon atom has the maximum number of hydrogens, then there is no trans fat. Fully hydrogenated (saturated) fats are now used, mixed with oils to get the proper hardness and softening range.

Other emulsifiers, such as lecithin, are sometimes used along with the skim milk. Colors are added (usually annatto or carotene) to get the right yellow color (uncolored margarine is white). Sometimes the milk is cultured with yogurt bacteria to get a stronger buttery flavor.

Some spreads are a mixture of margarine and butter, to achieve the flavor people like.

What gives people energy?

Energy is measured in calories. The three components of food that are responsible for most of the calories we consume are fats, carbohydrates, and proteins.

Fats have the most calories. Each gram of fat contains nine food calories. A food calorie is the energy needed to raise a liter of water by one degree Celsius. Non-food calories, the kind chemists and physicists use, are $1/1,000$ of a food calorie. A pound of fat contains over 4,000 food calories, enough to support a man for two days.

Carbohydrates are sugars and things made from sugars, such as starches. Carbohydrates contain 4 calories per gram, or just over 1,800 calories per pound—about a day's worth of calories.

Proteins also contain 4 calories per gram if they are burned in the body instead of used to make new proteins. If there is not enough energy in the other foods we eat, the protein will be burned for fuel. But much of the protein in a normal diet goes into building enzymes, skin, hair, muscle, and fingernails, some of which is lost every day and must be replaced.

Getting enough energy in your food is not the same as feeling energetic. You might feel most energetic in the morning before breakfast, when you haven't eaten for eight hours or more. Or some people may be addicted to the caffeine in their morning coffee and not feel energetic at all until after a cup or more of the stimulant.

So-called energy drinks take advantage of this confusion and contain both stimulants and lots of sugar. The stimulants wake you up and make your muscles overactive (jittery), which is often confused with being energetic.

Why do some medicines have flavor and others don't?

Some medicines taste awful by themselves. Medicines are compounds chemists have found to have an effect on our bodies. In many cases, they are small doses of poisons that plants, bacteria, or fungi have evolved to produce in order to kill whatever is eating them, by disrupting the attacker's internal chemistry.

Humans takes advantage of those millions of years of evolution by using small amounts of those poisons to change their body chemistry. But we humans have also evolved for millions of years alongside these other organisms, and we have evolved sensors in our tongues and noses to detect when something is poisonous. So many of our medicines taste awful, usually quite bitter.

We mask those bitter tastes by adding sugar and acids to overwhelm the tongue and by adding aromas and flavorings to overwhelm the nose. Even so, some flavored medicines still taste awful. And that is a good thing, because many are poisonous if too much is taken. You still want to be reminded that these things are dangerous if not used properly.

Why is bubble gum stretchy?

Bubble gum is stretchy because it is made of rubber. Natural rubber is made from the sap of the rubber tree. It is called latex, and it is a white sap similar to that of milkweed plants and dandelions. The word *gum* refers to the sap of plants, and gums are used for sealing envelopes and gluing things together.

Bubble gum and chewing gums these days are made from the sap of the *manilkara chicle* tree. The sap itself is just called chicle. It was once used as a substitute for natural rubber but is now mainly used for chewing gums. The name for one brand of chewing gum, Chiclets, comes from the word for the raw sap. A cheaper form of synthetic rubber is now used in many chewing gums.

Rubber and chewing gum are both examples of polymers, long chains of atoms strung together. The strings are tangled together and occasionally *cross-linked* so that one strand is connected to another, often in several places. This is what makes the rubber bounce back or pull together after being stretched. It is what gives something a rubbery, stretchy feel.

Why is there salt in almost everything you eat?

Because humans have evolved to crave salt.

Plants don't need sodium, but animals do. Since plants don't need it, they don't absorb it from the soil and they don't store it. As a result, animals that get most of their calories from plants need to find other things to eat that do contain sodium.

Some soils contain salt, and of course the ocean does. Animals have evolved taste sensors to tell them what things contain salt, and the brain has evolved to make eating salty things pleasurable so that animals will eat salty things, even if there is no other food value associated with them. Animals will walk miles to get to salt licks.

Humans are no different. We need salt, and our brains send pleasure signals when we get salt, just as we get pleasure from sweet things. And, just like sweets, people who make foods know that if there is more salt (up to a point) people will like the food more.

As the makers of food compete with one another for consumers' money, they find that consumers buy things that are saltier. Some food makers add salt so they can make more money.

Even at home, most people salt their food with more salt than they require in their diet, just because they have evolved to like the taste.

Why does sugar make you hyper?

It doesn't. The myth of sugar-induced hyperactivity has been disproven many times. But people continue to believe it, because situations that cause children to get excited, such as parties and holidays, are also situations where a lot of sugar is present. But in fact, the sugar may cause the most excitement before it is eaten, rather than afterward.

The parents of the children have been taught to expect hyperactivity due to sugar, and so when they see hyperactivity and sugar together, they infer a cause and effect. But when there is hyperactivity and no sugar present, they don't wonder that excitement can happen in the absence of sugar. This is similar to an effect called the full moon effect, named because nurses were once convinced that hospitals are busier during a full moon, despite records proving otherwise. The nurses would see a busy hospital and a full moon and associate the two. But when the hospital was busy when there was no full moon, they did not think to associate the lack of a full moon with the busy hospital.

Why do you get cavities when you eat too much sugar?

Actually, plain sugar doesn't stay in your mouth long enough to feed the bacteria that inhabit the film on your teeth. But foods such as dried fruits and many candies, which have sticky particles that slowly dissolve, will cause the bacteria to grow.

Your teeth are coated with a thin layer of material called plaque. This material is formed by bacteria in the mouth, which glue themselves to your teeth to avoid being swallowed. The bacteria eat sugar. When they eat the sugar, they produce acids. The bacteria do not eat your teeth, but the acids do dissolve tooth material if they accumulate enough to raise the acidity levels to a damaging level. It takes the bacteria about 20 seconds to convert sugar into acid, and the acid stays trapped in the plaque next to the teeth for about a half hour.

Soft drinks with sugar are more of a problem than plain sugar alone. First, they contain sugar. Second, they contain a lot of sugar. Third, they are consumed over a long period, so the sugar will feed the bacteria constantly. And lastly, they are more acidic than the acid the bacteria make from the sugar. Sour candies are similar— they contain high levels of acid that are more harmful to the teeth than the sugar they contain.

It is not the amount of sugar that is important, but how often you eat sugar. If you only eat it at mealtimes, the acids will be gone half an hour later. But if you sip a soda or a sugared coffee all day long, you will have a bigger problem, since the acid will be next to your teeth for many hours at a time.

Glossary

As Alexa read my answers to her questions, there were occasionally words that were unfamiliar to her. Some of the words I simply define here, but others are best explained by a more detailed examination of the concepts that they describe. So instead of a short a glossary item I will sometimes expand it into a longer explanation.

Albino An animal that lacks pigment (color) in the skin, hair, and eyes, making the skin and eyes pink and the hair white.

Alkali The opposite of an acid. In water, acids donate protons (a hydrogen atom that is missing its electron). Alkalis accept protons. Thus alkalis and acids neutralize one another in water, forming salts.

Bicarbonate The bicarbonate ion is a carbon atom with three oxygen atoms attached and a hydrogen attached to one of the oxygen atoms.

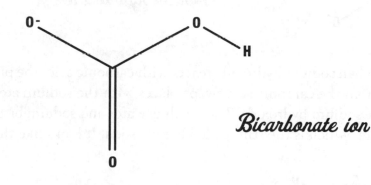

Bicarbonate ion

When carbon dioxide reacts with water, it forms carbonic acid.

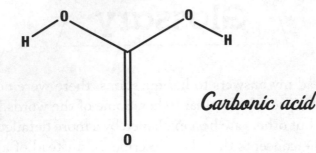

Carbonic acid

You can see the carbon dioxide in the molecule (the carbon and the two oxygens) and you can see the water (the two hydrogens and the third oxygen). Acids are things that easily lose a proton (a hydrogen atom without its electron). When carbonic acid loses a proton, it becomes a bicarbonate ion. You can see that the bicarbonate ion is missing the hydrogen nucleus (the proton), but it still has the electron. This gives it a negative charge. An alkali is usually what makes the acid give up the proton. Alkalis are proton-hungry molecules. One strong alkali is called sodium hydroxide.

Sodium hydroxide

When sodium hydroxide reacts with carbonic acid, the proton from the carbonic acid swaps places with the sodium atom in the sodium hydroxide. The result is water and sodium bicarbonate, which is the stuff called baking soda. It looks like this:

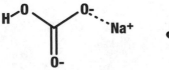

Sodium bicarbonate

Bipolar disorder A condition in which a person goes between being in a very good mood and a very bad mood, sometimes very quickly.

Chromatography A way of separating the molecules in a solution according to how well they travel in something like paper.

Capillaries Capillaries are the tiny blood vessels that bring oxygen and food to the cells in your body. Arteries are the larger blood vessels that pump the blood from the heart and lungs to the capillaries. Veins are the large blood vessels that take the blood from the capillaries back to the heart and lungs to get more oxygen.

Corrode To destroy or damage something by chemical reactions. When iron rusts, that is corrosion. When silver tarnishes, that is corrosion. A shiny copper penny becomes dull brown when it corrodes, and sometimes it can turn blue or green, depending on the type of chemical reaction causing the corrosion.

Catalyst A catalyst is something that helps make a chemical reaction go faster, without being used up itself in the reaction.

Delocalized electrons In some molecules, the electrons that form the bonds between the atoms are not stuck to just one atom or one bond but are shared between several atoms. Because they are not "local" to one bond, they are called *delocalized*.

Diluted Something is diluted (made less concentrated) by adding another substance to it, such as water. If someone's coffee is too strong, they might dilute it (make it weaker) by adding water.

Detonate To cause something to explode.

Dewar A big Thermos bottle. Long before the Thermos came on the market, James Dewar invented the concept behind it: a bottle inside a bottle, separated by a vacuum, as a way of keeping hot things hot and cold things cold.

Emollient   Something that softens or smoothes the skin.

Emulsifier   Something that helps oil and water mix into what we call an emulsion. An emulsifier is usually a molecule that has one end that attracts water and another end that does not. The molecules makes a coating around tiny drops of oil or water and keeps them from joining together to make larger drops.

Emulsion   A mixture of oil (or fat) and water, in which one of the substances is in the form of tiny droplets inside the other substance. Mayonnaise is an emulsion of oil in water. Butter is an emulsion of water in fat.

Ether   There are many kinds of ether, but the most common ones are liquids that are used to dissolve things that don't dissolve well in water or alcohol.

Diethyl ether

An example is diethyl ether, which is a liquid similar to alcohol, and it used to dissolve many organic chemicals such as fats and waxes. It is also sometimes used to make people sleep through operations in hospitals.

Equilibrium   An equilibrium occurs when opposing forces are balanced (equal). If you are balancing on a tightrope, you want to keep the forces that might tip you over equal on both sides, so you keep your equilibrium and don't fall off the rope. In chemistry, many reactions can be fairly easily undone. The forces that cause two molecules to join are fighting the forces that would cause them to separate. If some molecules are joining together at the same rate that other molecules are coming apart, the forces are said to be in equilibrium.

Friction   Friction is the resistance you feel when you rub two things together. Friction is what helps the brakes in a car slow the car down, and it is what keeps the wheels from sliding on the ground. The friction of a match sliding against the matchbook is what generates the heat needed to light the match.

Gallium   An element in the periodic table of elements. It is a metal that melts in your hand.

Gradient   A gradual change—for instance, a gradual change in voltage—that causes the things that are affected by it slide down it. A playground slide is a gravity gradient that causes you to slide down it, since you are affected by gravity.

Gypsum   Gypsum is calcium sulfate.

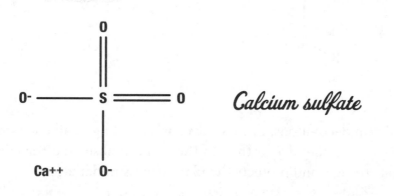

Calcium sulfate

It is the white rock inside sheetrock, the wallboard that many houses use to make their walls. It is similar in many ways to chalk.

Hemoglobin   Hemoglobin is the oxygen-carrying protein found in red blood cells. It is what makes blood with lots of oxygen look red and blood with little oxygen (such as that in the veins in your wrist) look blue.

Henna Henna is a plant that contains a molecule in its leaves called lawsone.

Lawsone is a reddish brown dye that binds strongly to proteins in skin, hair, and fingernails. It is used for temporary tattoos

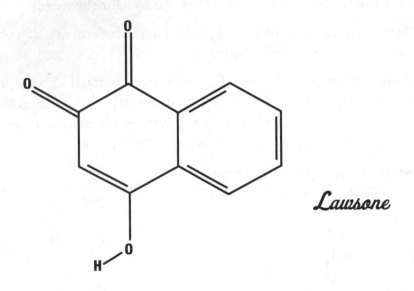

Lawsone

and skin decorations, as a hair dye, and as a fingernail colorant. It is also used to dye leather. In the plant, it absorbs ultraviolet light strongly and protects the plant from sun damage.

Infrared There is more to light than the rainbow of colors we can see. There is light that is beyond the red end of the spectrum, called infrared light, and there is light beyond the violet end, called ultraviolet light. Humans can't see either of these kinds of light. But we feel infrared light as heat, and ultraviolet light is what causes sunburns. There are other types of light beyond infrared, such as microwaves and radio waves. There are also other types of light beyond ultraviolet, such as X-rays and gamma rays.

Ionic   A substance (like table salt) that breaks up in water to form ions. Detergents are categorized as ionic surfactants (such as sodium lauryl sulfate) or nonionic surfactants (such as cetyl alcohol or polysorbates). Ionic surfactants work best in warm or hot water, while nonionic surfactants can work in cold water.

Linear   In a line. Molecules can be a linear string of atoms, or they can be a branching structure like a tree, or they can even have rings of atoms or complicated webs. But linear molecules are among the simplest types.

Lipase   An enzyme (a type of protein) that breaks down fat. It is used in digesting food. Fats and oils are called lipids, which is where lipase gets its name. Several other words that begin with *lip* also refer to fats. For example, a cosmetic surgeon might use a type of vacuum to suck fat out of a movie star, in a process called liposuction.

Lubricant   A substance, such as oil or grease, that is used to reduce friction. Cars use oils and grease to lubricate their parts, but people also use lubricants on their skin to reduce irritation caused by rubbing. Lubricants make things slippery.

Lubrication   Using or applying a lubricant to make something slippery.

Lye   Lye is the common name for sodium hydroxide, a powerful alkali used in many things, such as making soap out of fats. It is used in the home as a drain cleaner.

Microorganisms   Tiny (microscopic) little living things. Bacteria, algae, mildew, yeast, and tiny animals called protozoa, as well as tiny insects and similar animals that are too small to see are all organisms in the micro world, so we call them microorganisms.

Melanin   The main pigment in the skin and hair. It is what makes you tan, and it is what is missing in the gray hair of older people.

Mica Mica is a type of rock that forms very thin crystal sheets that look and feel like plastic. The flat sheets reflect light and are what makes the sand at the beach sparkle.

Monomer A molecule that links up with other monomers to form polymers, long chains of molecules. *Mono* means *one*, and *poly* means *many*.

Mucus Slime. Snails make it to walk on, and people make it in their noses to collect dust before it can get in the lungs. When you have a cold, it is what you sneeze into the tissue.

Olfactory cells The cells in your nose that detect odors and perfumes.

Opaque An opaque object or substance is something that completely blocks light. If you can see through something, it is transparent. If you can't see through it but light still comes through (like a thin piece of paper), we say it is translucent. But something like wood or metal that completely blocks the light is opaque.

Opium Opium is a drug made from a species of poppy flowers. Drugs made from opium are used to numb pain and to induce sleep.

Polymer See *monomer.*

Pores Small holes. We have pores in our skin so we can sweat and release oils to lubricate skin. Insects have pores in their skin so they can breathe. Plants have pores in their leaves so they can breathe. Something like a sponge, which has many pores and lets water through it, is called porous.

Rancid When foods containing fats or oils spoil, the oils combine with oxygen in the air to form bad-smelling and bad-tasting molecules. We say the food has gone rancid, which is just a way of saying that a fatty food has spoiled.

Reagent Something added in order to cause a chemical reaction or to see if a reaction happens.

Solvent A liquid that can dissolve something, Examples are water, alcohol, paint thinner, acetone, turpentine, and gasoline.

Soot Soot is the black stuff in smoke. It is made of tiny particles of carbon, the black element that gives charcoal its color. Almost any fuel that contains carbon can produce soot if there is not enough oxygen for it to burn completely.

Statins Statins are a type of drug used for reducing cholesterol in the blood of people, in the hope of reducing the risk of a heart attack.

Subtle Difficult to detect or describe, such as a subtle odor. So delicate or precise that it can be difficult to describe, such as a subtle difference between a California accent and a Colorado accent.

Surfactant A molecule such as soap, with one end that attracts water and one end that does not. A surfactant is active at the surface between oil and water and keeps droplets from coming together.

Thiol An organic (carbon-containing) molecule that contains a sulfur atom bound to a hydrogen atom. Thiols often have strong odors. The odor of garlic is due to thiols. Thiols are added to the gas used for cooking so that humans can detect the odor if there is a gas leak.

Voltage The pressure on electrons that make them flow. A 9 volt battery pushes electrons harder than a 1.5 volt battery.

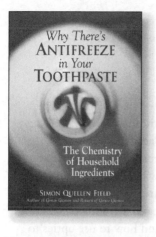

WHY THERE'S ANTIFREEZE IN YOUR TOOTHPASTE

The Chemistry of Household Ingredients

978-1-55652-697-8
$16.95 (CAN $18.95)

If you're like most people, you find it hard enough to *pronounce* the ingredients found in most household products, much less understand why they're there. No longer—with *Why There's Antifreeze in Your Toothpaste* you'll be able to distinguish between preservatives and sweeteners, buffers and emulsifiers, stabilizers and surfactants. Ingredients are grouped according to type, and each entry contains the substance's structural formula, synonymous names, and a description of its common uses. This helpful guide can be used as a basic primer on commercial chemistry or as an indexed reference to specific compounds found on a product label. Never fear the grocery again.

CULINARY REACTIONS

The Everyday Chemistry of Cooking

978-1-56976-706-1
$16.95 (CAN $18.95)

When you're cooking, you're a chemist! Every time you follow or modify a recipe, you are experimenting with acids and bases, emulsions and suspensions, gels and foams, and more. But unlike in a laboratory, you can eat your experiments to verify your hypotheses. *Culinary Reactions* turns measuring cups, stovetop burners, and mixing bowls into graduated cylinders, Bunsen burners, and beakers. How does altering the ratio of flour, sugar, yeast, salt, butter, and water affect how high bread rises? Why is whipped cream made with nitrous oxide rather than the more common carbon dioxide? And why does Hollandaise sauce call for "clarified" butter? This easy-to-follow primer even includes recipes to demonstrate the concepts being discussed.

Gonzo Gizmos
Projects & Devices to Channel Your Inner Geek

978-1-55652-520-9
$16.95 (CAN $18.95)

This book for workbench warriors features step-by-step instructions for building more than 30 fascinating devices. Detailed illustrations and diagrams explain how to construct a simple radio with a soldering iron, a few basic circuits, and three shiny pennies; how to create a rotary steam engine in just 15 minutes with a candle, a soda can, and a length of copper tubing; and how to use optics to roast a hot dog, using just a flexible plastic mirror, a wooden box, a little algebra, and a sunny day. Also included are experiments most science teachers probably never demonstrated, such as magnets that levitate in midair, metals that melt in hot water, and lasers that transmit radio signals.

Return of Gonzo Gizmos
More Projects & Devices to Channel Your Inner Geek

978-1-55652-610-7
$16.95 (CAN $22.95)

This fresh collection of more than 20 science projects—from hydrogen fuel cells to computer-controlled radio transmitters—is perfect for the tireless tinkerer. Its innovative activities include taking detailed plant cell photographs through a microscope using a disposable camera; building a rocket engine out of aluminum foil, paper clips, and kitchen matches; and constructing a geodesic dome out of gumdrops and barbecue skewers. Most of the devices can be built using common household products or components available at hardware or electronic stores, and each experiment contains illustrated step-by-step instructions with photographs and diagrams that make construction easy.

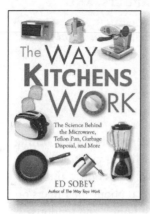

THE WAY KITCHENS WORK
The Science Behind the Microwave, Teflon Pan, Garbage Disposal, and More

Ed Sobey

978-1-56976-281-3

$14.95 (CAN $16.95)

If you've ever wondered how a microwave heats food, why aluminum foil is shiny on one side and dull on the other, or whether it is better to use cold or hot water in a garbage disposal, now you'll have your answers. *The Way Kitchens Work* explains the technology, history, and trivia behind 55 common appliances and utensils, with patent blueprints and photos of the "guts" of each device. You'll also learn interesting side stories, such as how the waffle iron played a role in the success of Nike, and why socialite Josephine Cochran *really* invented the dishwasher in 1885.

THE WAY TOYS WORK
The Science Behind the Magic 8 Ball, Etch A Sketch, Boomerang, and More

Ed Sobey and Woody Sobey

978-1-55652-745-6

$14.95 (CAN $16.95)

A Selection of the Scientific American Book Club

Profiling 50 of the world's most popular playthings—including their history, trivia, and the technology involved—this guide uncovers the hidden science of toys. Discover how an Etch A Sketch writes on its gray screen, why a boomerang returns after it is thrown, and how an RC car responds to a remote control. This entertaining and informative reference also features do-it-yourself experiments and tips on reverse engineering old toys to observe their interior mechanics, and even provides pointers on how to build your own toys using only recycled materials and a little ingenuity.

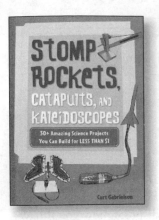

STOMP ROCKETS, CATAPULTS, AND KALEIDOSCOPES

30+ Amazing Science Projects You Can Build for Less than $1

Curt Gabrielson

978-1-55652-737-1

$16.95 (CAN $18.95)

There's no better way to understand how something works than to build it yourself. How does a toilet flush? Find out with a plastic drink bottle and a length of flexible tubing. What about the fingers on your hand? Construct a working model of their muscles, bones, and tendons using drinking straws, craft sticks, tape, and string. These and dozens of other hands-on projects can be found in *Stomp Rockets, Catapults, and Kaleidoscopes*. Each project has been designed to use recycled or nearly free materials. Kids will gain experience working with common tools and be encouraged to modify and improve their designs. Teachers will also appreciate the optional follow-up questions to gauge student understanding.

SODA-POP ROCKETS

20 Sensational Rockets to Make from Plastic Bottles

Paul Jarvis

978-1-55652-960-3

$16.95 (CAN $18.95)

Anyone can recycle a plastic bottle by tossing it into a bin, but it takes a bit of skill to propel it into a bin from 500 feet away. This fun guide features 20 different easy-to-launch rockets that can be built from discarded plastic drink bottles. After learning how to construct and launch a basic model, you'll find new ways to modify and improve your designs, including built-on fins, nose cones, and parachutes. More complex designs include two-, three-, and five-bottle rockets, gliding rockets, cluster rockets, whistling rockets, and a jumbo version made from a five-gallon water-cooler tank. Clear, step-by-step instructions with full-color illustrations accompany each project, along with photographs of the author firing his creations into the sky.

DOABLE RENEWABLES
16 Alternative Energy Projects for Young Scientists

Mike Rigsby

978-1-56976-343-8

$16.95 (CAN $18.95)

A Selection of the Scientific American Book Club

The earth's fossil fuels are being used up at an alarming pace, and once they're gone, they're gone. But other energy sources—solar, wind, waves, "waste" heat, and even human power—are both renewable and environmentally friendly. The projects in this book will help any budding scientist construct and explore working models that generate renewable, alternative energy. Readers will learn how to build a Kelvin water drop generator out of six recycled cans and alligator clip jumpers, a solar-powered seesaw from a large dial thermometer and a magnifying glass, and much more.

HAYWIRED
Pointless (Yet Awesome) Projects for the Electronically Inclined

Mike Rigsby

978-1-55652-779-1

$16.95 (CAN $18.95)

Written for budding electronics hobbyists, *Haywired* proves that science can inspire odd contraptions. Create a Mona Lisa that smiles even wider when you approach it. Learn how to build and record a talking alarm or craft your own talking greeting card. Construct a no-battery electric car toy that uses a super capacitor, or a flashlight that can be charged in minutes then shine for 24 hours. Each project is described in step-by-step detail with photographs and circuit diagrams, and helpful hints are provided on soldering, wire wrapping, and multimeter use.

Available at your favorite bookstore, by calling (800) 888-4741, or at
www.chicagoreviewpress.com

CHICAGO REVIEW PRESS